Pottermore Secrets
and Mysteries Revealed

The Unofficial Guide to
Pottermore.com

D1213666

h

POTTERMORE SECRETS AND MYSTERIES REVEALED: THE UNOFFICIAL GUIDE TO POTTERMORE.COM

ISBN-13: 978-0-7897-4942-0

ISBN-10: 0-7897-4942-4

The Library of Congress Cataloging-in-Publication Data is on file.

Printed in the United States of America

First Printing: December 2012

TRADEMARKS

WARNING AND DISCLAIMER

BULK SALES

Que Publishing offers excellent discounts on this book when ordered in quantity for bulk purchases or special sales. For more information, please contact

U.S. Corporate and Government Sales

1-800-382-3419

corpsales@pearsontechgroup.com

For sales outside the United States, please contact

International Sales

international@pearsoned.com

EDITOR-IN-CHIEF
Greg Wiegand

ACQUISITIONS EDITOR
Laura Norman

DEVELOPMENT AND TECHNICAL EDITOR
Jennifer Ackerman-Kettell

MANAGING EDITOR
Sandra Schroeder

PROJECT EDITOR
Mandie Frank

COPY EDITOR
Keith Cline

INDEXER
Cheryl Lenser

PROOFREADER
Jovana Shirley

PUBLISHING COORDINATOR
Cindy Teeters

DESIGNER
Anne Jones

COMPOSITOR
Studio Galou

CONTENTS AT A GLANCE

TABLE OF CONTENTS

ABOUT THE AUTHOR

Jason R. Rich (www.JasonRich.com) is the bestselling author of more than 54 books, including more than a dozen video and computer game strategy guides. In addition to being an accomplished photographer, he's also a frequent contributor to a handful of major daily newspapers, national magazines, and popular websites.

You can follow Jason on Twitter (@JasonRich7).

DEDICATION

This book is dedicated to J.K. Rowling, as well as to my niece, Natalie, and to my favorite Harry Potter fans, Emily and Ryan.

ACKNOWLEDGMENTS

Thanks to Laura Norman at Que Publishing for inviting me to work on this book and for all her guidance and patience as we've worked on this project. My gratitude also goes out to Greg Wiegand, Cindy Teeters, Jennifer Ackerman-Kettell, and everyone else at Que Publishing and Pearson Education who contributed their expertise, hard work, and creativity to the creation of *Pottermore Secrets and Mysteries Revealed: The Unofficial Guide to Pottermore.com*.

I also want to thank Frankie Donjae for his help in navigating my way through the online world of Pottermore.com.

WE WANT TO HEAR FROM YOU!

As the reader of this book, *you* are our most important critic and commentator. We value your opinion and want to know what we're doing right, what we could do better, what areas you'd like to see us publish in, and any other words of wisdom you're willing to pass our way.

We welcome your comments. You can email or write to let us know what you did or didn't like about this book—as well as what we can do to make our books better.

Please note that we cannot help you with technical problems related to the topic of this book.

When you write, please be sure to include this book's title and author as well as your name and email address. We will carefully review your comments and share them with the author and editors who worked on the book.

Email: feedback@quepublishing.com

Mail: Que Publishing
ATTN: Reader Feedback
800 East 96th Street
Indianapolis, IN 46240 USA

READER SERVICES

Visit our website and register this book at quepublishing.com/register for convenient access to any updates, downloads, or errata that might be available for this book.

HARRY POTTER GOES INTERACTIVE

What started off as an international bestselling book series has grown into a global phenomenon. The best way to experience Harry Potter's incredible adventures is to begin by reading the seven Harry Potter books, written by J.K. Rowling.

Then, you can relive Harry's adventures by watching all eight blockbuster movies. Each is available separately on DVD, as a digital download, or on Blu-ray and will keep you on the edge of your seat.

A Message from Your Owl

There's also a vast selection of Harry Potter-inspired toys, action figures, Lego® sets, puzzles, and traditional games, not to mention Halloween costumes, clothing, and fashion accessories designed for Harry Potter fans of all ages.

Plus, if you visit the Universal Studios Orlando theme park in Orlando, Florida, you can literally step into The Wizarding World of Harry Potter for a truly breathtaking and immersive experience. At this theme park, you get a whirlwind tour of the Hogwarts School of Witchcraft and Wizardry, a look at the Hogwarts Express, be able to walk through Diagon Alley, plus visit Ollivanders: Makers of Fine Wands.

If you happen to be in London, you can get a behind-the-scenes look at the making of the Harry Potter movies when you visit the Warner Bros. Studio Tour London – The Making of Harry Potter attraction.

Or if you're a gamer, you can take control of Harry Potter's adventures at home by playing a series of action-packed video and computer games that are available for the Xbox 360, PlayStation 3, Windows PC, Wii, and Nintendo DS.

After you get to know Harry, Ron, Hermione, Professor Dumbledore, Hagrid, Lord Voldemort, and the rest of the incredible, unusual, and often heroic characters within the Harry Potter series, there are so many different ways to relive their adventures and, in some cases, create your own.

A Message from Your Owl

One of the latest video game projects that J.K. Rowling is personally involved with is called *Wonderbook: Book of Spells* for the PlayStation 3. It enables you to read and actually experience what's inside the 200-year-old *Book of Spells*, which until now has been stored in the Restricted section of the Hogwarts library and available to select witches and wizards only.

And then, there's Pottermore! Anyone who can surf the Web, using a PC, Mac, or tablet, can visit **www.Pottermore.com** and experience Harry Potter's adventures in a unique and highly interactive way.

A Message from Your Owl

Keep in mind that some tablets (such as the Apple iPad) cannot display animations, which will limit what you can do during your visit to Pottermore. Other tablets, however, work with Pottermore just fine.

SO, WHAT'S POTTERMORE ANYWAY?

J.K. Rowling herself has teamed up with a group of talented website designers, game developers, artists, and other technological geniuses to create an online world based faithfully on the Harry Potter books. This unique website is called Pottermore.

A Message from Your Owl

Experiencing Pottermore.com is free. You can spend as much time as you want visiting and revisiting each area of Pottermore after you set up your very own account.

Pottermore isn't an eBook, but it does highlight important scenes from every chapter of the Harry Potter books, and it enables you to delve much deeper into those scenes by reading exclusive information that J.K. Rowling has written and added only to the Pottermore website.

You can also read detailed descriptions of characters, creatures, magical objects, and enchanted items, plus many of the locations that were featured within the Harry Potter books.

These descriptions reveal previously unreleased details and convey J.K. Rowling's personal thoughts and opinions, so you can discover things about Harry Potter's world that were not included within the original books or movies.

Plus, as you're making your way through Pottermore and experiencing each chapter of each book, two things happen at once. First, you follow in the footsteps of Harry, Ron, and Hermione and relive some of their awesome and magical adventures (in the order they happened within the Harry Potter books).

At the same time, however, your character within Pottermore has his own unique adventure, which you will help to control.

After establishing your Pottermore account, you have the chance to

- Obtain your own, unique magic wand from Ollivanders: Makers of Fine Wands.
- Select an animal avatar (an owl, cat, or toad) from Eeylops Owl Emporium & Magical Menagerie, which is located along Diagon Alley.
- Become a student at Hogwarts School of Witchcraft and Wizardry, put on the Sorting Hat, and be placed into Gryffindor, Ravenclaw, Hufflepuff, or Slytherin.
- Collect dozens of items during your exploration.
- Cast spells with your unique magic wand.
- Participate in the Wizard's Duel using your magic wand.
- Mix and brew magical potions.
- Earn house points based on your achievements and to help your house win the Pottermore House Cup.
- Share items and gifts with other Pottermore fans.
- Post your ideas and thoughts about Pottermore and the Harry Potter books so that other Harry Potter fans can discover what you think.
- Create and share your own Harry Potter-themed drawings and artwork.

Like the book series itself, Pottermore is divided into seven distinct areas, starting with Book 1, *Harry Potter and the Sorcerer's Stone*. Your online adventure begins in Book 1, Chapter 1, "The Boy Who Lived."

A Message from Your Owl

You aren't able to proceed beyond Book 1, until you've completed all 17 online chapters, which faithfully follow the *Harry Potter and the Sorcerer's Stone* book.

When Pottermore was first launched, only Book 1 was unlocked. Over time, each additional area within Pottermore will become available, giving you access to all new adventures and challenges.

For example, Book 2, *Harry Potter and the Chamber of Secrets* was unlocked on Pottermore in mid-summer 2012. Before you can access it though, you have to unravel all the mysteries and collect all the hidden items within Book 1 (which this unofficial strategy guide will help you do).

Wizarding Tip

After you've acquired your own magic wand and the ability to cast spells (which happens as you explore Book 1 online), you can then visit the Spells or Potions area of Pottermore at anytime to perfect your skills as a young wizard or witch, plus earn points for your house.

One of the things you can do within Pottermore is learn how to brew potions, after finding or buying all the necessary ingredients.

YOU CAN ALSO VISIT THE POTTERMORE SHOP

While you're visiting Pottermore.com, drop by the online-based Pottermore Shop. From here, you can purchase eBook versions of all seven Harry Potter books to read or reread on your digital eBook reader (such as your Kindle, Nook, or iPad).

The Pottermore Shop is also the only place you can purchase and download the digital audio editions for all seven Harry Potter books. With these audiobooks, you can listen to every word of each book and follow Harry Potter's adventures in yet another exciting and fun way.

A Message from Your Owl

You need a debit or credit card to purchase items from the Pottermore Shop online.

HOW TO NAVIGATE YOUR WAY AROUND POTTERMORE

To begin experiencing Pottermore for yourself, use any computer or tablet that has access to the Internet (with your parent's permission, of course) and visit **www.Pottermore.com**. The Pottermore home page is displayed.

Wizarding Tip

Use your mouse to move the onscreen cursor around on the Pottermore website. In some cases, the mouse cursor represents your magic wand, which you wave through the air to make things happen. If you're using a computer with a trackpad, move your finger around on the trackpad to move the onscreen cursor around.

Sign Up button   Sign In to Pottermore button

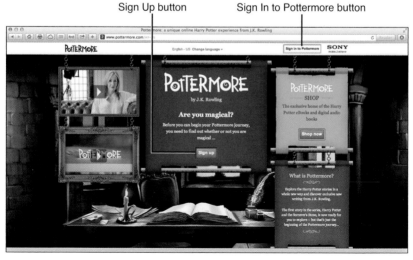

If this is your very first visit to Pottermore, click the Sign Up button that appears near the center of the home page.

If you're making a return visit, click the Sign In to Pottermore button, and then enter your username and password when prompted.

During your first visit to this unique website, you need to create your own unique Pottermore account. Click the Sign Up button. What to do next is explained later in this guide within Section II, "Signing Up for Pottermore.com."

You are then magically transported to Privet Drive, where your adventure officially begins. *Pottermore Secrets and Mysteries Revealed: The Unofficial Guide* walks you through every step of your adventure. This book helps you discover even the most difficult-to-find items, while giving you important clues about how to solve the puzzles you encounter and overcome the challenges you'll soon face.

Wizarding Tip

Don't forget, your Pottermore adventure follows each book in the Harry Potter series, chapter by chapter, so grab your copy of each book and read along as you make your way through your online-based adventure.

USE THE MAGICAL GATEWAY TO NAVIGATE YOUR WAY AROUND

Constantly displayed near the very top of the screen is the gateway. It consists of 10 circular icons plus the large Pottermore sign and your profile shield.

Perched on top of the Spells icon is the Messenger Owl. When you begin your adventure, the majority of the circular icons displayed within the gateway are locked. A lock symbol appears within most them, and when you click them, nothing happens.

Over time, as you work your way through Pottermore, new areas of the website are unlocked. By the time you're done with Book 1, *Harry Potter and the Sorcerer's Stone*, nine of the icons will be unlocked: Diagon Alley, Gringotts, Great Wall, Common Room, Spells, Potions, Trunk, Friends, and Favorites.

After an icon on the gateway is unlocked, click it to immediately access that area of Pottermore. For example, click the Trunk icon at anytime to display the contents of your trunk. This is where all the items you collect during your adventure are stored.

A Message from Your Owl

A bit later, you discover where you wind up after clicking each of the other unlocked icons that are displayed within the gateway.

At anytime, click the Pottermore title that shows near the top center of the screen to view the entire magical gateway.

Sorcerer's Stone icon

Chapter dots   Profile Shield   Pottermore title

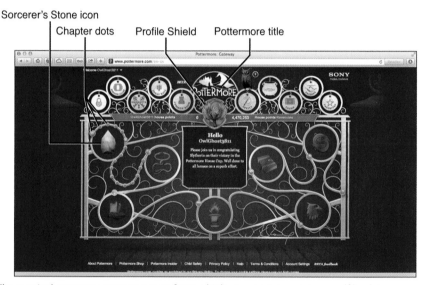

The magical gateway serves as a map from which you can transport yourself back to any scene within any chapter of any book you've already completed within Pottermore.

During your first visit to Pottermore, only Book 1, Chapter 1, "The Boy Who Lived," is unlocked on the magical gateway. Book 1's icon, which by no coincidence looks like the Sorcerer's Stone, is displayed near the top-left corner. By the time you've completed Book 1, all 17 of the chapter dots are gold colored and clickable.

Wizarding Tip

Click a chapter dot that's displayed within the magical gateway once to reveal a chapter title, or double-click to enter into that chapter.

A Message from Your Owl

Each circle within the magical gateway represents one of the Harry Potter books. The dots around each circle, and the dots that connect the seven circles, each represent a chapter of a particular book.

VIEW YOUR PROFILE PAGE

When you first start your adventure, the icon below the Pottermore title looks like a silver shield. Click it to view your unique profile page at anytime.

A Message from Your Owl

After the Sorting Hat has assigned you to a house, the shield's appearance changes. It will ultimately display your house's color and insignia. This happens during your experience in Book 1, Chapter 7, within Pottermore.

Your profile page reveals information about your Pottermore character and her accomplishments.

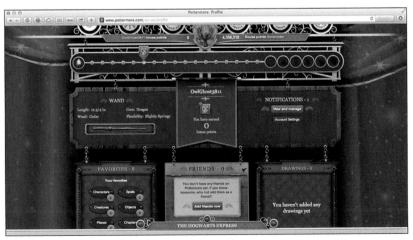

As you progress through your adventure, the information within your profile page changes.

Your profile page is divided into several sections. Along the top of the screen, just below the gateway, a progress meter shows how far along you are in a particular Pottermore adventure. You can click any dot, each of which represents a chapter you've completed, to return to that chapter. The rightmost dot on the progress meter represents the chapter you're currently exploring. Click it to return to where you left off in your adventure.

A Message from Your Owl

After the Sorting Hat has assigned to you a house, how many house points you've personally earned is shown just below the gateway on the left side of the screen. To the right of that, on the opposite side of the profile shield, is the total number of house points your house has earned.

Near the top left is (or will be) information about your unique magic wand. Near the top center are (or will be) details about how many house points you have personally earned. Near the top right of the profile page is a listing of any notifications you've received, either from the Pottermore website operators or from your online friends and fellow Pottermore users.

When you scroll downward a bit on your profile page, you find a Favorites section. A listing of the characters, spells, creatures, objects, places, chapters, and potions you've tagged as your favorites are accessible.

Remember, from each chapter introduction or chapter summary screen during your adventure, as well as anytime you unlock information about something new within Pottermore, you can click the Favorites button and add it to your Favorites list.

One of the great things about Pottermore is that you can meet friends online who are Harry Potter fans, just like you! If one of your real-life friends is also on Pottermore, you can meet online, as long as you know your friend's unique username. Or while you're exploring Pottermore, you can meet and interact with new friends online.

Wizarding Tip

Some of the ways you can interact with other people include being able to post public comments, send and receive gifts, or challenge others to a Wizard's Duel. You learn more about these aspects of Pottermore a bit later.

Access information about your Pottermore friends from the Friends section of your profile page, or simply click the Friends icon at the top of the screen within the gateway.

A Message from Your Owl

You learn all about how to meet friends on Pottermore from Section VI, "Making Friends with Fellow Witches and Wizards in Pottermore," later in this book.

Another thing you can do on Pottermore is share your artistic talents with others by uploading your drawings and artwork to the Pottermore website, where it will be displayed for all to see.

You can also view galleries of other people's art. From your profile page, you can manage the drawings that you've uploaded to Pottermore. You learn how to upload and share your drawings from Section VII, "Your Adventure Continues."

The bottom three sections of your profile page allow you to view and access your inventory of spells and spell books, potions, and your trunk. During your adventure, you unlock new spells and potions. However, you can also learn how to cast new spells and mix new potions on your own.

Wizarding Tip

Section IV, "Wizard's Duels: Enhance Your Spell-Casting Skills," helps you become a master at casting spells and winning Wizard's Duels.

Also, be sure to check out Section V, "Potion Brewing for Hogwarts Students," to learn all about how to find or buy the ingredients you need to brew your own potions.

RECEIVE MESSAGES FROM THE OWL

Perched quietly atop the Spells icon on the gateway throughout your adventure is a dark-colored Messenger Owl with bright orange eyes. If a number appears within a circular icon next to the owl, this indicates you've received a message, either from the Pottermore website operators or from one of your online friends. To access the message, click the owl.

Notifications from the Messenger Owl can include the following:

- Friend requests from others
- Acceptance notices for friend requests you've sent
- Information about gifts others have sent you
- Challenges from other people for a Wizard's Duel
- Results of a Wizard's Duel challenge
- News about online events, such as the Pottermore House Cup
- Important messages from the creators of Pottermore

Wizarding Tip

You can also access incoming messages (and respond to messages from your friends) by clicking the Friends icon within the gateway or by clicking the View and Manage button under the Notifications heading on your profile page.

EXPERIENCE POTTERMORE CHAPTER BY CHAPTER

After your adventure begins, you discover that each book within Pottermore is divided into chapters. Each chapter consists of two or three separate scenes.

Before each chapter, you see a chapter introduction page. It offers a preview of the scenes you'll soon experience, plus the chance to add a particular area of Pottermore to your Favorites list.

As soon as you finish each chapter, a chapter summary screen reveals useful information and helps you keep track of where you are and what's happening at that point in your adventure.

Throughout your adventure, a banner appears near the bottom center of the screen. It includes the name of the scene you're currently in.

As you're looking at the banner, click the left-pointing arrow next to it to move back to the previous scene. Click the right-pointing arrow on the opposite side of the banner to advance to the next scene.

By waving your mouse over the upward-pointing arrow near the top center of the banner, you can display a short description of the scene you're in.

MANAGE YOUR POTTERMORE ACCOUNT

After you've set up your Pottermore account, you can access the Account Settings options to update or change your information, such as your email address, country, language of choice, or your password.

On the Account Settings page within Pottermore, you can manage your account after setting it up.

You can access the Account Settings page in any of these three easy ways:

- Click your username near the top-left corner of the Pottermore screen and select Account Settings from the pull-down menu.

- Access your profile page and click the Account Settings button under the Notifications heading on the right side of the screen.

- Click the Account Settings link at the bottom of the Pottermore website.

Magical Warning

From the Account Settings page, you can also delete your Pottermore account. However, if you click the Delete Account button on the Account Settings page, and then confirm your decision by clicking the Yes, Delete My Account Now button, your Pottermore account is erased forever.

As a result, all your account-related information, including your unique username, wand, avatar animal, what house you are assigned to, and all your items, are lost.

A FEW MORE MENU COMMANDS ARE AVAILABLE TO YOU

At anytime, if you scroll down to the bottom of the Pottermore page you're on, you discover a handful of links, including the following:

- **About Pottermore**: Read a brief description about what the Pottermore website is all about.

- **Pottermore Shop**: Access the Pottermore Shop to purchase Harry Potter eBooks and digital audio books.

- **Pottermore Insider**: Read the official online blog written by the creators of Pottermore. Discover what's new on the site and read important announcements.

- **Child Safety**: Read basic tips that help you stay safe when communicating with people through the Pottermore website. Also, be sure to read Section VI for more information about communicating with your online friends.

- **Privacy Policy**: Discover what happens to the personal information you provide when you create a Pottermore account or make purchases from the Pottermore Shop.

- **Help**: If you have a question about Pottermore, chances are you can find the answer within this book. However, you can also check out the Help section of the website.

- **Terms & Conditions**: A group of lawyers who represent J.K. Rowling and Pottermore put together this long legal document that's full of fine print about what you can and cannot do on the Pottermore website. Don't worry; you can skip reading this section and go right to experiencing your adventure.

- **Account Settings**: Click this link to gain quick access to your Account Settings page while visiting Pottermore.

YOUR ADVENTURE IS ABOUT TO BEGIN

Now that you know the basics for navigating your way around Pottermore, you're ready to start your interactive adventure. The next section of this book walks you through the Pottermore account setup process. Then, within Section III, "Your Magical Adventure Begins," you discover everything you need to know to successfully make your way through all of Book 1, *Harry Potter and the Sorcerer's Stone.*

Thanks to Pottermore and all that it offers, there's never been a more exciting time to be a Harry Potter fan. Just like Harry has done, you now have an opportunity to make your mark on the wizarding world by showcasing your skills as a witch or wizard as you encounter countless challenges.

Say goodbye to your days living as a muggle, and get ready to experience a magic-filled life as a wizard or witch who is a student at Hogwarts School of Witchcraft and Wizardry.

Good luck!

IN THIS SECTION

- Register to Be a Hogwarts Student
- Follow in Harry's Footsteps, but Experience Your Own Adventure as Well
- Choose Your Pottermore Username and Password
- Discover if You, too, Are Magical

SIGNING UP FOR POTTERMORE.COM

F or one very special young boy named Harry, his magical wizarding adventure began on Privet Drive in the most unusual of ways. After all, Harry was raised as a muggle by his aunt and uncle. He grew up not knowing that his parents possessed incredible magical powers or that his destiny was to become one of the greatest wizards who ever lived.

Your magical adventure and education at Hogwarts School of Witchcraft and Wizardry can begin in your own home, or anywhere you have a computer or device that can connect to the Internet. But like all up-and-coming wizards and witches, you need to apply to become a student at Hogwarts and discover firsthand if you, too, are indeed magical.

From any computer or tablet with a web browser, visit www.Pottermore.com. Near the center of the screen, look for this question: Are you magical? Click the Sign Up button.

REGISTER TO BE A HOGWARTS STUDENT

The Hogwarts admission process involves five steps. To complete Step 1, answer this question: When were you born? Using the onscreen pull-down menus, select the day, month, and year of your birth, and then click Continue.

To become a student at Hogwarts, answer five questions.

Step 2 requires you to tell the Admissions Department at Hogwarts what country you live in. Use the pull-down menu to select the United States (or wherever you live). Click Continue to move to Step 3.

Wizarding Tip

Near the top center of the screen, click the Change Language option to select your native language. Your choices include English (US), English (UK), Spanish, French, Italian, or Dutch.

For a truly authentic Pottermore experience, select English (UK) as your language. After all, J.K. Rowling is British, and she wrote the Harry Potter books in her native language.

Now it's time to introduce yourself. When you reach Step 3, enter your first name and last name in the proper fields. Then, click the Male or Female option. You're also asked to enter your email address. (If you don't have your own email address, ask your parents if you can use theirs.)

A Message from Your Owl

When you are experiencing Pottermore, your name, age, and email address are kept private. However, the Pottermore website needs to know who you are and be able to send you important emails to you about your adventure.

If you're under the age of 13, you have to provide a parent's email address, so he can give you permission to visit Pottermore and set up your own account.

Magical Warning

One of the best things about experiencing your adventure on Pottermore is that you can share it with other Harry Potter fans. However, whenever you're posting public comments, never reveal your real name, age, address, email address, what school you attend, the names of your brothers or sisters, or any other personal information about yourself.

As soon as you register at Hogwarts School of Witchcraft and Wizardry on Pottermore, you receive a really special and one-of-a-kind username. Not only will you use this username to sign in to Pottermore from now on, but it is also how you are known to your online friends while you're experiencing Pottermore.

As you move on to Step 4, you create a super-secret password that you use to access Pottermore in the future. Your password must be at least six characters long and include at least one number. Select whatever password you want, but make sure you write it down and remember it.

Your Attention Please...

If you accidently forget your password, don't worry. Go to the Pottermore sign-in screen. Below the Please Enter Your Password field, click the Forgotten Your Password? option. You're be asked to enter your username. The Pottermore website sends you an email message to remind you of your password.

If you forget your username, click the Forgotten Your Username? option below the Please Enter Your Username field. Enter the same email address you used to register for Pottermore in Step 3. You receive an email message to remind you of your Pottermore username.

In Step 5, you are asked which Harry Potter books you've read and which of the movies you've seen. Using the mouse, click the check box for each book you've read and for each movie you've seen, and then click Continue. If you're a true Harry Potter fan and have read all the books or maybe you've seen all the movies (or have done both), click either or both the All options at the bottom of the list.

CHOOSE YOUR UNIQUE POTTERMORE USERNAME

Congratulations! Your application for admission to the Hogwarts School of Witchcraft and Wizardry is finished. You have been chosen for admission because you too are magical. Click Continue to receive your very special username.

You select your Pottermore username while viewing this screen.

On the left side of the screen, under the Please Choose Your Username heading, five choices for your Pottermore username appear.

After you select a username, you cannot change it. Instead of being known by your muggle name, from now on, when you're experiencing your magical adventure on Pottermore, you're known by the username you select. Choose wisely.

On the right side of the screen, within the empty field, enter the two words in the box that's displayed. (What's displayed might not be real words that muggles use, but you should enter them exactly as you see them into the empty field.)

Next, confirm that your email address is correct, and then click Create My Account.

YOUR ADMISSION LETTER COMES BY EMAIL, NOT BY OWL

Although Harry and other soon-to-be students typically receive messages from Hogwarts via owl, your letter from Hogwarts comes via email, so check your inbox.

Your Username will be displayed here.

Your email address will be displayed here.

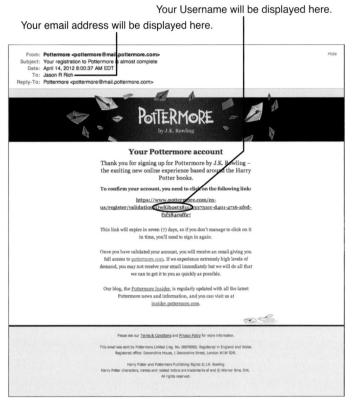

Within a few minutes (or hours), you receive a confirmation email that your application to Hogwarts School of Witchcraft and Wizardry is pending.

The first email you receive from Pottermore includes a validation link. It's important that you click this link within 7 days of receiving the email to confirm your information.

When you click the link within your confirmation email, your computer's web browser opens, and you're asked to sign in to your Pottermore account using your brand new username and the password you created. Enter your password where it says Please Type in Your Password to Explore Pottermore. Then, click Sign In to Pottermore.

Your Pottermore account is now officially validated. You're just one step away from starting your magical adventure.

Now, you have need to wait for Pottermore to send you a Welcome email. However, it could take a few hours or even a day or two for this important email to arrive. Be patient, but check your email account's inbox regularly so that you don't miss it.

Your own personal Pottermore Username will be displayed here.

The second email you receive tells you that "The World Of Pottermore Awaits." You are reminded of your username. Your Pottermore.com account is now ready. Your adventure and exploration can finally begin.

From your computer or tablet's web browser, visit www.Pottermore.com, and click Sign In to Pottermore near the upper-right corner of the screen. Enter your username and password, and then click Sign In. Your next stop is Privet Drive.

Wizarding Tip

To save time in the future when signing in to Pottermore, use the mouse to click the check box located next to the Keep Me Signed In option. When you do this, your web browser remembers your username and password. Then, you won't have to reenter this information every time you visit Pottermore.

A Message from Your Owl

After you begin your adventure, you can change your Pottermore account settings at anytime. For example, you can change your email address, password, or language choice. You can also delete your account altogether.

You can access the Account Settings page in several ways. Check out Section I, "Harry Potter Goes Interactive," for details on how to do this.

After you sign in to Pottermore for the first time, your adventure kicks off in with Book 1, *Harry Potter and the Sorcerer's Stone*, Chapter 1, "The Boy Who Lived."

FOLLOW IN HARRY'S FOOTSTEPS, BUT EXPERIENCE YOUR OWN ADVENTURE AS WELL

From this point forward, two things happen while you're experiencing Pottermore. You relive some of Harry's adventures, and as a Hogwarts student, you also experience some of your own unique challenges and have the opportunity to find and collect items, cast spells, brew potions, and earn house points for the house that the Sorting Hat assigns you to.

In fact, you are also given your own unique magic wand, can select your own pet, and the Sorting Hat places you into a house that might or might not be Gryffindor.

Remember, what happens to your character during your adventure might be different from what Harry, Ron, or Hermione experienced in the Harry Potter books, but that's part of what makes Pottermore truly exciting.

Wizarding Tip

You earn house points by successfully brewing potions, casting spells, and participating in Wizard's Duels. On an ongoing basis, your house, whether Gryffindor, Ravenclaw, Hufflepuff, or Slytherin, needs to collect as many house points as possible to win the Pottermore House Cup. Every point you earn helps your house toward winning this important prize.

IN THIS SECTION

- Begin Your Pottermore Adventure
- Discover Items, Potions, Characters, and New Places
- Read Exclusive New Information from J.K. Rowling
- Experience Harry's the Adventure in *Harry Potter and the Sorcerer's Stone* in a Whole New Way

111

YOUR MAGICAL ADVENTURE BEGINS

One aspect of your Pottermore.com online adventure follows each chapter of each Harry Potter book, starting with *Harry Potter and the Sorcerer's Stone*.

Pottermore.com Secrets and Mysteries Revealed includes everything you need to know to work your way through the entire first book, plus become an expert at casting spells when participating in Wizard's Duels and when brewing potions.

Just like Harry Potter himself, your adventure kicks off on Privet Drive. Soon, however, you're visiting Diagon Alley and Gringotts to gather up all the items you need to begin your studies at Hogwarts School of Witchcraft and Wizardry.

Everything you experience as you work your way through your adventure follows what happens in the Harry Potter books. However, not everything happens just like it did to Harry. Based on how you respond to challenges and questions, the Sorting Hat decides which house to place you in as your witch or wizard training begins. Then, some aspects of your adventure are totally unique. Plus, your ability to duel and mix potions relies on your own personal skills.

Even if you've read the Harry Potter books and have seen the movies, you're about to encounter many surprises and challenges that put your magical abilities to the test.

Wizarding Tip

As you explore each chapter of *Harry Potter and the Sorcerer's Stone* on Pottermore.com, you visit many familiar locations from the books and movies. Within each location, you collect specific items and place them within your trunk for safekeeping.

As you progress through your adventure, some of the items you discover are needed later. So, if you forget to pick up an important item, you might have to return to a location to find and retrieve it. When you need an item you've already found, just open your trunk and grab it.

Also, hidden within the various places you visit are galleons. This is the money you use to buy school supplies and items needed for mixing potions, for example. So, when you discover a galleon, be sure to grab it.

THE MAGICAL GATEWAY

A magical iron gate serves as your entranceway to the online world of Pottermore. Because you're magical, opening the gate is easy. The area of the gate you click the mouse on determines where you wind up within your adventure.

The circle near the upper-left corner of the gate is the entranceway to *Harry Potter and the Sorcerer's Stone.* Click it to begin your adventure. As you complete chapters during your adventure, they are unlocked and become accessible from the gateway.

Each circle within the gateway serves as a portal to one of the Harry Potter books.

A Message from Your Owl

When you place your computer's mouse over the icon for *the* first book, if the title that appears says *Harry Potter and the Philosopher's Stone*, this means you've selected English (UK) as your language when setting up your account. You can change this easily to English (US) by locating your username in the upper-left corner of the screen and clicking it. Then, from the menu, click Account Settings.

When looking at the Account Settings page, click the Edit button below the Personal Details heading. For the Your Language of Choice option, choose English (US), and then click the Save button.

Click the Pottermore title near the top of the screen to return to the Magical gateway.

CHAPTER 1: THE BOY WHO LIVED

Chapter 1 of Pottermore.com begins at the beginning of the *Harry Potter and the Sorcerer's Stone* book. You find yourself on Privet Drive. It's nighttime. On the dark street, all you see is a lonely cat and an old parked car.

Remember, while exploring any of the scenes in Pottermore, you can double-click the mouse to zoom in or double-click again to zoom out. Unless you zoom in on certain characters, creatures, or objects, you aren't able to interact with them, even if they're visible.

Wizarding Tip

Another way to zoom in or out of a scene is to use the up- or down-arrow keys on the keyboard. You can press the up-arrow key once or twice, depending on how much you want to zoom in, and then press the down-arrow key once or twice to zoom back out.

SCENE 1: NUMBER FOUR, PRIVET DRIVE

As you're looking at the magical gateway, click once on the Chapter 1 icon for *Harry Potter and the Sorcerer's Stone* to enter Pottermore.com. When the small Chapter 1: The Boy Who Lived window opens, click the Explore Chapter 1 button. You are then magically transported to Privet Drive.

Every chapter begins with an introduction screen. It tells you where you are in the story and how many scenes you're exploring. Here in Chapter 1, Scene 1 is called "Number Four, Privet Drive." Scene 2 is called "Something Peculiar Is Happening," and Scene 3 is called "Harry Is Delivered." Click the Explore Chapter 1 button to begin.

A Message from Your Owl

As you're working your way through your exciting Pottermore adventure online, you can follow along by reading the Harry Potter books. You discover that each of the chapters and scenes within Pottermore follow each chapter of each book in order. So, when you open the book *Harry Potter and the Sorcerer's Stone,* Chapter 1 is called "The Boy Who Lived," just like on Pottermore.

At the beginning of this scene within Pottermore, a series of pop-up windows explain what's about to happen. After you read the text within each window, click the right-pointing arrow on the right side of the window to continue.

In this case, after reading what's in the four windows, click the X in the upper-right corner of the last window to enter into the scene and begin your exploration.

Welcome to Privet Drive! Using a bit of technological wizardry, you find yourself transported to the street where the Dursley's house is located.

Of course, you remember Harry's Aunt Petunia Dursley, Uncle Vernon Dursley, and cousin Dudley Dursley. Harry has been living with them since he was a little boy, but as we quickly discover, nobody is too happy about the living arrangement.

A Message from Your Owl

At the bottom of the screen, you see the scene title banner. It's surrounded by a left-, right-, and up-arrow icon. Wave your mouse over the left arrow and click to return to the previous scene. Place your mouse over the right arrow and click to proceed to the next scene. Or to read a short description of the scene you're in, wave your mouse over the up-arrow icon.

Move the mouse around to explore Privet Drive and look for hidden items to gather.

Wizarding Tip

Wave your mouse over the cat's tail to make it move. Wave your mouse over the car's rear lights to turn on the windshield wipers and lights. Did you hear the car's horn honk?

Now's a good time to click the Privet Drive street sign to "discover" this location. A pop-up window enables you to access new information about Privet Drive that comes directly from J.K. Rowling herself. Click the New from J.K. Rowling button to read this exclusive information.

After you've discovered something new, you can then wave your mouse over the Places icon on the left side of the screen under the Read About sign, and then click the Number Four, Privet Drive listing to read the content from J.K. Rowling.

When looking at any Places screen that's full of new details from J.K. Rowling, click the Back button to return to your adventure. You find it near the upper-left corner of the screen.

Your Attention Please...

By scrolling to the bottom of any Read About screen, you can share your own thoughts and ideas about Pottermore by adding a comment. You can also "like" other people's comments.

Up arrow icon

CHAPTER 1

NUMBER FOUR, PRIVET DRIVE

When Mr. and Mrs. Dursley woke up on the dull, gray Tuesday our story starts, there was nothing about the cloudy sky outside to suggest that strange and mysterious things would soon be happening all over the country...

NUMBER FOUR, PRIVET DRIVE

A scene title banner is always visible. Here, the mouse is placed over the up-arrow icon to make this scene description appear as well.

When you're done exploring any scene, click the right arrow near the bottom center of the page. You find it to the right of the scene title banner. This transports you to the next scene. Wave your mouse over the up arrow icon to read a description about the scene you're in.

SCENE 2: SOMETHING PECULIAR IS HAPPENING

This scene also takes place on Privet Drive. Now, however, you find yourself standing directly outside of the Dursley's house.

Put-Outer

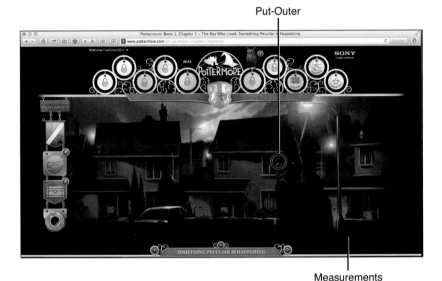

Measurements

Spend a few minutes exploring this area of Privet Drive carefully.

Hidden here are a few important items. Oh, and by the way, that's none other than Professor Dumbledore hiding in the shadows under the streetlight!

A Message from Your Owl

Don't forget, you can learn all about the various characters you encounter in Pottermore by waving your mouse over the Characters icon that's along the left side of the screen under the Read About sign.

Wave your mouse over the Characters icon to display a Characters menu that lists the characters you've discovered in that scene. Click any of the character's names, like Professor Dumbledore.

Move the mouse over the Places icon to see a menu of places you've visited to learn more about them.

Harry Potter's world is filled with magical and enchanted items. To learn more about the items you discover during your adventure, wave your mouse over the Objects icon below the Places icon, and then click an object's listing to learn more about it.

continues

When you're a witch or wizard, creatures play an important role in your life. Throughout his adventure, Harry encounters many exotic creatures—some friendly, some magical, and some that are rather dangerous. To learn more about the creatures you come across during your Pottermore adventure, wave your mouse over the Creatures icon. You find it below the Objects icon.

Some characters, places, objects, and creatures that are listed under the Read About sign need to be found and unlocked. However, you also discover some information that's listed here appears automatically.

Wizarding Tip

Click Professor Dumbledore's put-outer (in his hand) to make it light up for a few seconds. This gadget, which looks like a lighter, is used to magically turn off the lights along Privet Drive.

Here on Privet Drive, when you click the base of the streetlight on the right side of the screen, you unlock the Measurements object.

To read about the Measurements object, click the New from J.K. Rowling button that appears. You discover that witches and wizards do not use the metric system to measure things. They have their own measuring system, which for them works just fine. Later, to reread details about measurements, click the link for it on the left side of the screen when you wave your mouse over the Objects icon (which looks like a trunk).

SCENE 3: HARRY IS DELIVERED

As you enter into this new scene, you discover that an owl remains perched at the top of your gateway. He brings you important notifications related to Pottermore.com. Can you see the owl hiding among the icons near the top of the screen, just above the Spells icon? At anytime, click the owl to access the Notifications page.

Now, look up in the sky. It's a flying motorcycle! Hagrid rides it to get around. Zoom in on the motorcycle and on Hagrid to get a closer look.

Aside from clicking the motorcycle to hear its engine roar, there's not too much to do here.

A Message from Your Owl

Each time you enter into a new scene, the Read About information available to you (by waving your mouse over the Characters, Places, Objects, or Creatures icons) will change.

In some cases, new entries are featured. Plus, additional information under entries you've already unlocked in previous chapters might be updated with new and interesting information.

Place your mouse over the right-pointing arrow at the bottom of the screen to make the Chapter 1 summary screen appear. From this screen, you can read a recap of what's happening in the story, click links that you unlocked to access special content from J.K. Rowling, plus you can add a comment of your own that other Pottermore fans are able to read.

A Message from Your Owl

While reading any chapter summary screen, click the Add to Favorites icon if you want to save this as one of your favorite Pottermore scenes. You can also like a scene or chapter by clicking the Like icon. To return quickly to any of your favorite places, click the Favorites icon on the right side of the gateway (at the top of the screen).

When you're ready to move on, click the right-pointing arrow near the bottom of the screen, next to the scene title banner. After reading the introduction screen for Chapter 2, click Explore Chapter 2 to enter into the first scene of this chapter.

Your Attention Please...

Did you know that while visiting Pottermore.com you can purchase the Harry Potter books in eBook format (which you can then read on your computer screen or using an eBook reader)? Plus, you can purchase, download, and listen to the Harry Potter audiobooks. To do this, from the chapter summary screen, click the Pottermore Shop link. To make purchases from this online store, you have to use a credit card or debit card.

If your Pottermore account is registered in the United States, you can only purchase the U.S. editions of the Harry Potter eBooks and audiobooks.

CHAPTER 2: THE VANISHING GLASS

For almost 10 years, Harry has been living with the Dursleys, totally unaware of his magical powers, but all that is about to change.

Like every new chapter in Pottermore, Chapter 2 begins with an introductory page that offers a preview of the scenes you're about to explore firsthand. As you see from the preview images near the center of the screen, Chapter 2 includes two scenes. Click the Explore Chapter 2 button near the center of the page to continue your adventure.

Wizarding Tip

It's here in Chapter 2 that you start collecting items that you store in your trunk during your adventure. These are items that you might want or need to use later. At anytime, to view the contents of your trunk, click the Trunk icon on the right side of the gateway.

As you make your way through your Pottermore adventure, more and more of the icons displayed within the gateway unlock and new Pottermore features are revealed.

The gateway is constantly displayed at the top of the screen. Right now, the majority of the icons on the gateway remain locked, except for Trunk, Friends, and Favorites.

SCENE 1: THE CUPBOARD UNDER THE STAIRS

Most young people have their own bedroom or share a bedroom with their brothers or sisters. The Dursleys didn't give Harry his own bedroom. Instead, he slept in a small storage space under the staircase. It doesn't look too comfortable, does it?

Start looking for the items hidden here. As you explore this area of the Dursley's home, remember that you can double-click the mouse (or use the up-arrow and down-arrow keys) to zoom in and out on certain areas or to look more closely at specific items. For example, zoom in and look at the picture frame on the small table near the staircase.

Wizarding Tip

When you click the picture frame near the staircase, a pop-up window says, "You've unlocked Vernon and Petunia Dursley." Click the New from J.K. Rowling button to read more about these popular characters.

This is what "The Cupboard Under the Stairs" scene looks like when you first enter into it. You need to zoom in, however, to see everything that's important.

Now that you've unlocked the information about the Dursleys, you can click the Vernon & Petunia Dursley listing under the Characters heading on the left side of the screen to learn more about Harry's aunt and uncle.

Next, zoom in twice on the doorway near the small area under the staircase to get a closer look (or press the up arrow twice). Do you hear that ticking sound?

Wizarding Tip

Tick, tick, tick. Sounds like an alarm clock. Look for the clock on the floor. Zoom in to see and click it. Congratulations! You've discovered your first item: the alarm clock. Click the Collect button to store this newfound treasure within your trunk.

SCENE 2: THE TRIP TO THE ZOO

From *Harry Potter and the Sorcerer's Stone*, do you remember one of the first times Harry discovered he had magical powers and could communicate with animals? It happened during a trip to the zoo.

When you're exploring the zoo, the key to discovering everything within this exhibit is to zoom in on the various cages and to wave your mouse over objects or creatures that look interesting.

Wizarding Tip

Zoom in on the cage to the right and wave your mouse over it to see a lizard crawl up the tree.

Next, zoom in again and click the large snake cage near the center of the screen. To reach this boa constrictor, you need to zoom in twice from the point where you first entered the scene.

Use your magical powers to wake up the snake and look directly into his eyes. Don't be afraid, between you and the scary-looking boa constrictor is a clear, solid, and thick glass wall. Or is there?

Wave your mouse over the sign to the right of the snake. A Closer Look button appears. Click it to learn more about this boa constrictor. Click the X in the upper-right corner of the Boa Constrictor window to make it disappear.

When you finished exploring the zoo, move your mouse to the bottom of the screen and click the right-pointing arrow next to the banner that now reads "The Trip to the Zoo."

Read the Chapter 2 summary screen, and when you're ready, click the right-pointing arrow next to the chapter title banner at the bottom of the screen. It now says "The Vanishing Glass." You can now begin Chapter 3.

CHAPTER 3: LETTERS FROM NO ONE

From the Chapter 3 introduction screen, click the Explore Chapter 3 button to enter the first scene. It's called "Harry Receives a Mysterious Letter."

At this point, Harry's aunt and uncle were very unhappy with him after what happened at the zoo.

Back at the Dursley's home, Harry receives a mysterious letter. It wasn't delivered by a postman, however.

SCENE 1: HARRY RECEIVES A MYSTERIOUS LETTER

Someone has written Harry a letter. Well, actually, a lot of letters were sent. This marks the first time someone has ever sent Harry a letter. The young wizard-to-be was excited, confused, and curious, all at the same time.

As you watch a handful of letters magically fly around, take a few minutes to explore the Dursley's kitchen. See what else you can find.

Click the letter sitting on the kitchen table.

Look on the kitchen table. You discover a salt and pepper shaker that you can click. Be sure to click the Collect button to add these items to your trunk.

On the refrigerator door, there's a postcard. Zoom in and click it. This, too, is an item you want to look at closely and then store in your trunk. Click the Collect button that appears when you move your mouse over the postcard. When the You've Found the Postcard pop-up appears, click the Collect button again. The message "This item has been added to your trunk" displays.

Next, zoom in again and look through the door behind the table. On the floor, you see a hammer and nails. Click them and add them to your trunk.

Wizarding Tip

At first, when Harry received his letter, his aunt and uncle tried to hide it from him. So, using a bit of magic, the mysterious sender delivered a few more letters. Well, actually, a lot of letters. Wave your mouse over the fireplace to see what showed up at the Dursley's house.

Remember that at anytime you can see what's already stored within your trunk. Click the Trunk icon within the gateway. So far, you've collected the alarm clock, hammer and nails, a postcard, and the salt and pepper shakers.

Click the chapter title banner at the bottom of the screen to return to the scene you were in. Then, when you're ready, click the right-arrow icon next to the banner that says "The Hut on the Rock" to move on.

A Message from Your Owl

In between the scenes "Harry Receives a Mysterious Letter" and "The Hut on the Rock," a message appears reminding you to check out your profile page. Click the X in the upper-right corner of this window to continue.

SCENE 2: THE HUT ON THE ROCK

Standing on land, you can look out into the water and see the waves crashing along the shoreline. It's nighttime, and the wind is howling.

Do you see a small hut on an island in the middle of the water?

When you first enter this scene, click the seashells over to the right. You want to collect the shells and place them in your trunk.

Wizarding Tip

Near the bottom center of the screen, hover the mouse over the hermit crab to make him crawl around a bit.

Now, take a closer look at the hut. Zoom in twice. Examine the rock on which the hut is sitting. Be sure to click the seaweed to collect it. It's hard to spot, so keep your eyes peeled. After collecting the seaweed, wave your mouse over the hut to turn on the light. Is anyone home?

When you're ready to move on, click the right-pointing arrow next to the banner that says "The Hut on the Rock."

Once again, a chapter summary screen appears. Click the right-arrow icon next to the "Letters from No One" banner to exit the Chapter 3 summary page and view the Chapter 4 introductory page.

CHAPTER 4: THE KEEPER OF THE KEYS

The days of Harry living as an ordinary muggle are about to end! It turns out that Hagrid is inside the hut on the rock. He's ready to take Harry with him on an adventure. From the Chapter 4 introduction page, click the Explore Chapter 4 button to continue your adventure and exploration.

A Message from Your Owl

By clicking the Like button of a chapter summary or chapter introductory page, you can add your vote to the ever-growing number of Harry Potter fans who also enjoyed this area of Pottermore.

SCENE 1: HAGRID ARRIVES

It's a dark, rainy, and thundery night. Lurking in the shadows by the door is a massive figure. Who could this be? It's Hagrid, of course. He's come to pick up Harry.

The door that was keeping the wind and rain outside is torn off its hinges as Hagrid enters the room. Hover your mouse over the light bulb that's hanging from the ceiling. Watch as it swings back and forth.

This scene takes place inside the hut.

Be sure to search the fireplace mantle to the right. Click the candle and collect it. You definitely want to add this item to your trunk.

Also, look around carefully near Hagrid's feet, over to the right. There are some papers on the floor. Zoom in and click them. A Read About button appears. When you click these papers, you reveal and unlock the Ghost Plots. Click the New from J.K. Rowling button to read about them right now, or you can click the Ghost Plots listing under the Characters heading of the Read About banner.

Whenever you unlock something new, a pop-up message congratulates you. Be sure to click the New from J.K. Rowling button to read exclusive information about the item you've unlocked.

SCENE 2: HARRY RECEIVES HIS LETTER AT LAST

Harry is about to experience the most amazing birthday of his life. He finally gets to read the mysterious letter that arrived and was addressed to him. From this letter, he discovers details about his parents, his past, and what's in store for his future.

Wave your mouse over the light bulb to make it swing. Sitting on the couch, next to the birthday cake, is a letter addressed to Mr. H. Potter. Hover the mouse over the letter and click the Closer Look button to read what it says.

As Harry reads his letter, he discovers that he's been invited to study at Hogwarts. Before classes begin, however, he needs to stock up on a ton of supplies. Hagrid ultimately invites Harry to Diagon Alley for a shopping experience he won't soon forget. To close the letter, click the X in the upper-right corner of it.

Wizarding Tip

As you explore this room, zoom in once and wave the mouse over the door to make it open and close.

On the floor near the fireplace, be sure to check out the small cup. (You need to zoom in once from where you first entered the scene to grab this item.) You discover it's a chipped cup. Click the Collect button and add it to the contents of your trunk.

Wizarding Tip

When you hover your mouse over the hotdogs that are cooking in the fireplace, you see them sizzle. Then, wave your mouse over the candles sitting on the fireplace mantle. Doing this makes them light up or blow out.

When you're ready to move on, click the right-pointing arrow next to the "Harry Receives His Letter at Last" banner. It's located near the bottom center of the screen. Next, you see the Chapter 4 summary screen.

Continue on your quest by clicking the right-arrow icon next to "The Keeper of the Keys" banner near the bottom center of the screen.

What happens next in your adventure not only impacts what happens to Harry but also influences the rest of your own personal magical adventure.

CHAPTER 5: DIAGON ALLEY

A lot happens here in Chapter 5, both to Harry and to you. As every witch and wizard knows, Diagon Alley is they place to shop for the very best magical supplies and items available.

During this particular visit to Diagon Alley, you adopt a pet (an owl, cat, or toad) from the Eeylops Owl Emporium & Magical Menagerie, plus you visit Ollivanders: The Makers of Fine Wands. There, you receive your very own magic wand.

SCENE 1: ARRIVING AT DIAGON ALLEY

Follow the cobblestone streets and make your way through the hustle and bustle of the crowds as you begin exploring Diagon Alley.

You soon head into a few of the shops to buy the important items needed by new students who will be attending Hogwarts.

There are many shops along Diagon Alley. However, you cannot enter into all of them yet. Make your way forward by zooming in on the scene.

Look to the left and click the storefront doors. You discover clothing. When the Read About button appears, click it. Then, after seeing the "You've discovered 'Clothing' by J.K. Rowling" message, click the New from J.K. Rowling button to read some exclusive content.

Be sure to look on the ground for a sheet of paper. When you find it, pick it up. Printed on this paper is your shopping list. It tells you all the items you need to purchase during this visit to Diagon Alley.

For example, you need your uniform, books, a few other items (like a cauldron, telescope, brass scales, and a set of glass or crystal phials). Oh, and you can't leave Diagon Alley without your magic wand and your new pet.

But first, Harry needs galleons so that he can buy all the items on his list.

SCENE 2: HARRY AND HAGRID VISIT GRINGOTTS

Before you and Harry can start buying the items on the shopping list, your immediate goal is to find Gringotts and to withdraw some galleons. As you explore Diagon Alley, you can find this legendary bank straight ahead.

Wizarding Tip

Gringotts is located within a large white building. When you see it at the end of the street, zoom to automatically enter into the bank. Much to your surprise, an account is already open for you.

A Message from Your Owl

The money you spend in Pottermore.com is called galleons. Your Gringotts bank account has all the galleons you need to buy everything on your shopping list. However, as your exploration continues, you want to collect additional galleons so that you can buy more items later. You can find hidden golden galleons within many of the places you'll soon be visiting.

As soon as you enter into Gringotts for the first time, the Gringotts icon that's part of the Pottermore gateway (at the top of the screen) unlocks. It's the third icon from the left. From this point on, you can click the Gringotts icon at anytime to return here.

Gringotts is a very secure building with lots of safes. To access your galleons, you must unlock your safe. Drag the golden key that appears directly over the lock.

Gringotts icon

To access your money, drag the golden key downward onto the lock using your mouse.

From the main Gringotts Wizarding Bank screen, you can view your current balance (which is 500 galleons). Click the Go to Diagon Alley button on the left to return to Diagon Alley and start shopping.

As soon as you leave Gringotts, you can review your shopping list more closely and figure out what you need to buy (and from which stores). When you're ready, click the Go Shopping button.

SCENE 3: HARRY GOES SHOPPING

As soon as you're back on the streets of Diagon Alley, you discover that it's easier to navigate your way around. The crowds seem to have thinned out a bit, and the area is much calmer.

Now, when you pass your mouse over each storefront, you can see the name of the store. Click a store's front door to go inside and shop.

On the left side of Diagon Alley, closest to where you're standing, is Potage's Cauldron Shop. If you check your shopping list, you see that you need to drop in here to buy a size 2 pewter cauldron.

Wizarding Tip

Near the upper-right corner of the screen, you see a Shopping List button. Click it at anytime to review the list of items you need to shop for. Then, click the Go Shopping button or the X on the shopping list to return to Diagon Alley.

When you enter any store along Diagon Alley, including Potage's Cauldron Shop, you see many items on display, along with their prices.

According to your shopping list, you need one size 2 pewter cauldron. It costs 15 galleons. Click the item to view a detailed description of it. Then, click the Buy button to purchase it.

After your purchase is completed, click the Back button near the upper-left corner of the window. After you make sure that there's nothing else from the store you need (based on what's on your shopping list), click the Exit Shop button in the upper-left corner of the store's page.

Located to the right of Potage's Cauldron Shop is the Apothecary. From here, you want to stock up on items needed to create potions. Later, when you begin your potion mixing studies, you need to return here often to buy more supplies. Right now, however, you don't need anything from the Apothecary.

Shopping List button

To the right of the Apothecary is Wiseacre's Wizarding Equipment.

Drop into Wiseacre's Wizarding Equipment to buy some of the items on your shopping list, such as the brass scales, telescope and the glass or crystal phials.

After you're inside Wiseacre's Wizarding Equipment, start by clicking the brass scales on the left side of the screen to purchase it for 3 galleons.

Read the description for the brass scales and make sure it matches up with the item listed on your shopping list. Click the Buy button. Then, click the Back button to return to the main store.

This time, click the brass telescope. View the item, click the Buy button, and then click the Back button once again.

Wizarding Tip

Refer back to the shopping list by clicking the Shopping List button once again near the upper-right corner of the Wiseacre's Wizard Equipment store screen. You discover that the items you've already purchased from the list have been crossed off. However, from this shop, you still need to buy the glass or crystal phials.

As you're browsing through Wiseacre's Wizarding Equipment, click either the glass phials or crystal phials to view the item description. Glass phials cost 3 galleons, and crystal phials cost 7 galleons. Either item is ideal for holding potions. Pick one of the phial sets and purchase it.

Right now, it doesn't matter if you purchase glass or crystal phials. Later, as you become skilled at brewing potions, certain recipes specifically require glass or crystal phials, so ultimately, you'll need to buy both.

When you're done shopping here, exit out of the store.

A Message from Your Owl

Also on the right side of Diagon Alley is Florean Forescue's Ice Cream Parlor and Madam Malkin's shop. However, at this point in your adventure, these destinations remain locked. In the future, when you return to Diagon Alley, these shops might be open.

On the right side of Diagon Alley, starting closest to you, you discover Flourish and Blotts. This is the bookstore where you buy all the magic and spell books needed for Hogwarts, like *A History of Magic and Magical Theory*. When you enter this shop, check your shopping list for a complete list of books you need to buy. According to your shopping list, you have eight different books to buy.

Start with *The Standard Book of Spells (Grade 1)* and continue buying one book at a time until they're all crossed off your shopping list. So, you also need to buy *A History of Magic*, *Magical Theory*, *A Beginner's Guide to Transfiguration*, *One Thousand Magical Herbs and Fungi*, *Magical Drafts and Potions*, *Fantastic Beasts and Where to Find Them*, and *The Dark Forces: A Guide to Self-Protection*.

Exit out of Flourish and Blotts after buying all the required textbooks.

Magical Warning

Be sure to check your shopping list one last time before you leave the Flourish and Blotts bookstore. Make sure you didn't forget any of the books. If you forget to buy an item from your shopping list, you have to return to buy that item before you can leave Diagon Alley.

Located to the left of Flourish and Blotts is Quality Quidditch Supplies. You can't enter into this store just yet. However, to the left again is Eeylops Owl Emporium & Magical Menagerie. This is where you soon select your pet. You can choose between an owl, cat, or toad.

NEXT STOP, EEYLOPS OWL EMPORIUM & MAGICAL MENAGERIE

It's time to choose your new pet, who serves as your loyal and loving avatar animal in Pottermore. Enter into Eeylops Owl Emporium & Magical Menagerie. It's a really awesome pet store for wizards and witches. You find it on the right side of Diagon Alley.

Inside Eeylops Owl Emporium & Magical Menagerie, several shelves display individual cages. Within each cage is one animal. The selection here is extensive. Click the More Pets button on the right side of the screen to view even more exotic owls, cats, and toads.

Remember, a wizard or witch can have only one special pet, so choose your favorite.

A Message from Your Owl

The animal you pick represents you whenever you post a comment on Pottermore.com. Plus, your pet is also displayed on your profile page and follows you throughout the rest of your Pottermore.com adventure.

Out of all the animals available from Eeylops Owl Emporium & Magical Menagerie, choose your absolute favorite and click its Buy button.

Magical Warning

After you purchase one animal from Eeylops Owl Emporium & Magical Menagerie, you can continue to browse through the store, but you aren't able to buy another pet or exchange the one you've purchased. All sales are final, so think carefully before you click an animal's Buy button.

After adopting your pet, there's only one more item to buy on your shopping list. You still need your very own, one-of-a-kind magic wand that's selected just for you!

Exit Eeylops Owl Emporium & Magical Menagerie and return to Diagon Alley. Notice that the entranceway to Diagon Alley South Side is now unlocked.

Wizarding Tip

After you've purchased the majority of the items from your shopping list from the stores along Diagon Alley, click the gold arrow in the middle of the street. You can then walk past Gringotts Wizarding Bank and check out the shops along Diagon Alley South Side.

A Message from Your Owl

Displayed below the Pottermore gateway icons near the top-left side of the screen, look for a golden icon that says Galleons. A number appears within it. This number indicates how many galleons remain within your Gringotts bank account. When you spend money, your balance goes down. When you find galleons, the balance goes up.

The very best place to go wand shopping is Ollivanders: Makers of Fine Wands. This famous store is located along Diagon Alley South Side. To get to it, click the gold right-pointing arrow that appears near the center of the street.

Diagon Alley South Side features a handful of additional shops, like The Daily Prophet, Whizz Hard Books, Second-Hand Robes, The Junk Shop, Obscurus Books, Gamol and Japes, and Twilfit and Tattings.

PURCHASE YOUR MAGIC WAND AT OLLIVANDERS: MAKERS OF FINE WANDS

At this point in your adventure, most of the shops along Diagon Alley South Side are closed. However, located in the center of the alleyway is Ollivanders—your next destination. Click the doorway to go inside.

To make sure you wind up with a magic wand that's perfect for you, Mr. Ollivander asks you seven questions. After reading the message that appears when you enter the store, click the Let Your Wand Choose You button.

A Message from Your Owl

That magic wand that's selected for you at Ollivanders: The Makers of Fine Wands is the one you use later in your adventure for dueling. Every wand is selected specifically for its owner. Or, more accurately, the wand selects you. You are asked a handful of questions as part of the wand-selection process. Be sure to answer each question as honestly as you can.

Let's take a quick look at just three of the possible questions you might be asked as Mr. Ollivander selects your own personal and unique wand.

Wizarding Tip

There are no right or wrong answers, but how you answer Mr. Ollivander's questions determines which wand you wind up with as your very own. As you answer each question, don't think about how Harry would respond. Instead, answer each question based on your own thoughts.

The first question you're asked is "Would you describe yourself as…." Your three options for answers are these:

- Short for your age
- Average height for your age
- Tall for your age

Click your answer to highlight it. Next, click the Next Question button.

You might be asked about the day you were born and need to inform Mr. Ollivander if it was on an odd-number or even-number day. So, if you were born on July 7, for example, that would be an odd number. But, if you were born on December 6, that would be an even number. Figure out if your own birthday falls on an even or odd number.

For odd-numbered birthdays (these days of the month: 1, 3, 5, 7, 9, 11, 13, 15, 17, 19, 21, 23, 25, 27, 29, and 31), click the card displayed on the left.

For even-numbered birthdays (these days of the month: 2, 4, 6, 8, 10, 12, 14, 16, 18, 20, 22, 24, 26, 28, and 30), click the card displayed on the right.

Some of the questions require you to make a decision.

Sometimes, witches or wizards need to make important decisions. The decisions they make later impact the events that happen in their lives. To test your decision-making skills, Mr. Ollivander might ask a question like this:

> Traveling alone down a deserted road, you reach a crossroads (a split in the road). Do you continue… Left, toward the sea? Ahead toward the forest? Or, right toward the castle?

Take a look at the map on the screen and choose one destination.

When you finish answering Mr. Ollivander's questions, you are given the chance to change any of your answers. Remember, how you answer each of these questions determines which wand you receive. Now, you can start again and re-answer each of the seven questions and change one or more of your answers. Or, you can click the Get Your Wand button to receive your magic wand. The decision is yours.

Congratulations! Your unique wand has been selected. This is the wand you use as you progress through your adventure and then participate in duels. The wand you receive might look totally different from the one shown here. That's because your wand is unique.

By now, you should have everything you need to begin your education at Hogwarts. At this point, return to Diagon Alley and finish up Chapter 5. To do this, click the right-arrow icon at the bottom of the screen, next to the "Ollivander's" banner. The Chapter 5 summary screen will appears.

You always have the option to view your profile page. To do this, click the silver Shield icon up in the gateway (near the top center of the screen).

Wizarding Tip

At anytime, to view your profile page, from the gateway, click the Shield icon directly below the Pottermore title near the top center of the screen. From your profile page, you can do the following:

- View your wand.
- See how many house points you've earned.
- View your Pottermore username and avatar animal.
- Read notifications.
- Check out the areas of Pottermore you've labeled as your favorites.
- View drawings you've posted on Pottermore.
- Review spells.
- View your available potions.
- Access the contents of your trunk.
- Take a closer look at other items you've collected so far in your adventure.

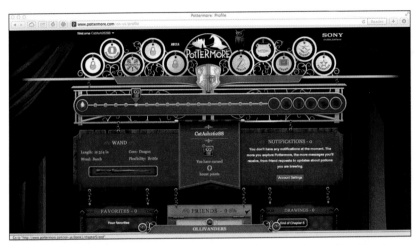

Let's take a moment and check out your profile page. After you've been placed in a house within Hogwarts, your house's insignia replaces the Shield icon on the gateway.

Wizarding Tip

Each time you accomplish something new within Pottermore, your profile page is updated automatically.

You've successfully completed Chapter 5. You've accomplished a lot so far, but so much more magic and mystery awaits you. Now, Harry must wait until September 1, when he boards the train at King's Cross and makes his way to Hogwarts for the very first time. But, your adventure within Pottermore.com can continue right now!

If you look at the gateway icons near the top of the Pottermore screen, several more of them have now been unlocked, including Diagon Alley, Gringotts, Spells, Potions, Trunk, Friends, and Favorites. Click any of these icons to transport yourself to that location or screen within Pottermore.

You can also click the Shield icon (displayed below the Pottermore title) to view your profile page. The Messenger Owl continues to be perched on the Spells icon. Click him to view any messages you've received from friends or from the Pottermore.com website.

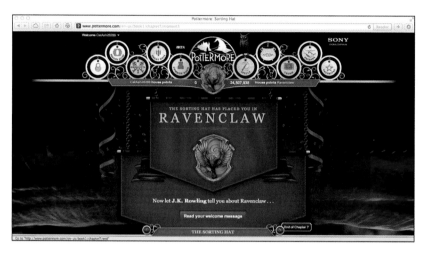

New gateway icons have been unlocked.

A Message from Your Owl

Do you think you know everything there is to know about the world of Harry Potter? Well, guess again! As you make your way through your adventure, you unlock exclusive new information from J.K. Rowling.

From a chapter summary page, you can view the new content headings you've unlocked. In Chapter 5, for example, you've unlocked Clothing, Mr. Ollivander, Wand Cores, Wand Lengths & Flexibility, and Wand Woods. Before moving on, take a few minutes to read this information.

Also, some of the entries for the Characters, Places, Objects, and Creatures you unlocked earlier in your adventure might have been updated, so check to see what's new there as well.

If you don't want to read everything that's new right now, you can add individual pages to your collection of favorites and then easily return to read those entries later.

Before moving on, post your own Comments about Pottermore.com in the Comments section displayed farther down on the chapter summary page.

If you decide to take a break from Pottermore and want to return to your adventure later, picking up where you left off is easy: just pass through the magical gateway.

A Message from Your Owl

If you exit out of Pottermore.com and return later, you might need to reenter your Pottermore password. When you sign in to Pottermore. com, add a check mark to the Keep Me Signed In option on the Sign In To Pottermore screen so that your username and password is remembered.

At this point in your adventure, if you take a look at the gateway screen, you see that around the *Harry Potter and the Sorcerer's Stone* icon that Chapters 1 through 6 have already been unlocked.

Click the Chapter 6 dot to enter back into Pottermore and pick up at the beginning of this next chapter, where you last left off.

CHAPTER 6: THE JOURNEY FROM PLATFORM NINE AND THREE-QUARTERS

This chapter begins when Harry is about to leave the Dursleys and hop aboard the Hogwarts Express. His next stop is Hogwarts. Chapter 6 has two scenes: "The Hogwarts Express," and "The Journey to Hogwarts." Click the Explore Chapter 6 button to begin this part of your adventure.

SCENE 1: THE HOGWARTS EXPRESS

At the train station, Harry has figured out how to enter platform nine and three-quarters. The train has already arrived, and everyone's luggage is being loaded.

As you explore platform nine and three-quarters, you see a handful of cats and owls; some are in cages, others are roaming around freely. Wave your mouse over them to hear them purr or hoot. Also, if you run your mouse over one of the packages near where you're standing (to the left of some textbooks), a strange creature attempts to crawl out.

Before boarding the Hogwarts Express train, explore platform nine and three-quarters.

Now, if you look slightly to the right, you see a bag with a purple object lying against it. Wave your mouse over the object. When the Collect icon appears, click the object. You discover the prefect badge. Add this item to your trunk.

Zoom in once. Above the passengers' heads and to the left, you see a sign. When you wave your mouse over it, a Read About button appears. Click the button. The sign says "The Hogwarts Express."

Next, look down and straight ahead. Listen for the sound of a toad croaking. Find the toad and click it. He's hiding near the center of the screen, to the left of the Hogwarts Express engine. When you click the Read Me button next to the toad, you unlock Toads.

Wizarding Tip

Did you know that toads are one of three approved pets that Hogwarts allows students to have? By unlocking Toads, you can click the New from J.K. Rowling button to read more about these creatures.

Or, after you've unlocked Toads, wave your mouse over the Creatures icon on the left side of the screen (under the Read About sign), and choose the Toads option.

Zoom in one more time. This time, when you look up and to the left, you see a second sign. Wave your mouse over it to reveal a Read About button. Click it to discover "Platform Nine and Three-Quarters." To read exclusive information, click the New from J.K. Rowling button.

SCENE 2: THE JOURNEY TO HOGWARTS

For all Hogwarts students, the trip aboard the Hogwarts Express is a time to meet up with old friends and to be introduced to new students. It's also a great time to start collecting chocolate frog cards.

As the Hogwarts Express train races toward Hogwarts School of Witchcraft and Wizardry, take a few minutes to explore. The train car you're riding in contains several interesting items to be found.

Wizarding Tip

One way to learn all about famous wizards and witches, like Professor Dumbledore, is to collect chocolate frog cards. Throughout Book 1 of your adventure, there are 11 cards for you to find and collect. From this point forward, keep on the lookout for them.

On the floor, there's a large trunk. Click it to open the trunk and see what's inside. Surprise! You just discovered the Dumbledore chocolate frog card. Click the Collect button to add it to your collection. Now, you only have 10 more chocolate frog cards to find and collect!

Wizarding Tip

You discover the Morgana chocolate frog card sitting on the right seat of the train car, near the arm rest. Click it, as well, to collect it.

Zoom in and wave your mouse slowly over the tabletop in the train car. You find and are able to collect Bleaaargh, a sprout-flavored bean. Also, when you wave your mouse over the open book that's on the table, the pages turn. Plus, when your mouse passes over the right curtain, a tiny creature pops its head out to greet you.

Soon, the Hogwarts Express arrives at its destination. The passengers unload and follow Hagrid to the main castle door of Hogwarts.

CHAPTER 7: THE SORTING HAT

For every new Hogwarts student, putting on the Sorting Hat and being assigned to a house is a huge deal. Like all the other new Hogwarts students, you're about to be sorted and placed into a house, where you remain for your entire adventure.

What do you think? Will you be placed into Gryffindor, Hufflepuff, Ravenclaw, or Slytherin? Unfortunately, that decision isn't up to you. It's for the Sorting Hat to decide. In Pottermore, the Sorting Hat chooses a house for you, based on how you answer a series of questions.

SCENE 1: THE ENTRANCE HALL

Chapter 7, "The Sorting Hat," includes three scenes. First, you arrive at Hogwarts. Then, you participate in the sorting ceremony. Finally, you are placed into one of the four houses. Just like in the *Harry Potter and the Sorcerer's Stone* book, after the Sorting Hat places you into a house, the decision is final, and that's the house where you remain as long as you continue playing Pottermore using the same account.

The Entrance Hall at Hogwarts is massive and quite beautiful. Be sure to take a close look at the staircase as you explore. On the fourth step from the bottom, you find and are able to collect your first galleon. This gives you extra spending money when you visit Diagon Alley again later.

Wizarding Tip

Zoom in once and wave your mouse over the large wooden doors on the right to make them open and close.

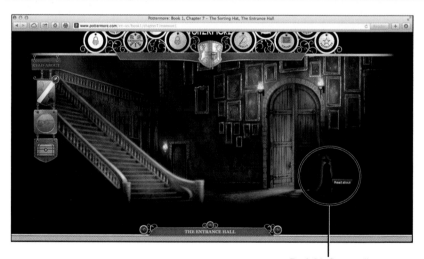

Prof. McGonagall

Welcome to Hogwarts!

After zooming in to take a closer look at the wooden doors, move your mouse slowly around in the area to the right of the large wooden doors. You come across Professor McGonagall lurking in the shadows and are able to unlock some new information.

After you've unlocked the information about Professor McGonagall, click the New from J.K. Rowling button to learn more. You discover the entry about this Hogwarts-educated witch has been updated from earlier.

Wizarding Tip

When you exit from this area of Hogwarts by clicking the right-arrow icon next to "The Entrance Hall" banner, kick back and watch a short video starring J.K. Rowling. She explains more about the Sorting Hat.

SCENE 2: THE SORTING CEREMONY

The time has come for you to step up to the Sorting Hat and discover which house you'll become a lifetime member of. After watching the J.K. Rowling video, click the Try On the Sorting Hat button to begin the Sorting Ceremony.

The Welcome to Hogwarts page is displayed next. You're instructed to answer a series of questions to help the Sorting Hat place you into the proper house. Click the Begin button to continue.

You're asked a series of questions, to which there are no right or wrong answers, so answer honestly.

Wizarding Tip

During your adventure, which questions you get asked by the Sorting Hat vary.

The following are three possible questions you might be asked before the Sorting Hat makes a decision about which house to place you in.

Question:

> You're given a choice to invent a potion. What would be the purpose of the potion you invent? Click the cards to make your selection. Here, your choices include: Love, Glory, Wisdom, or Power.

Click the Select This Option button on the card that displays your selection. Then, click the Yes, Please Proceed button to continue.

Here's what another question might be:

> If a troll were to wreak havoc in the headmaster's study and try to destroy what's inside, in which order would you protect the following items: Merlin's Book, Hogwarts student records (that go back 1,000 years), and the dragon pox cure.

Using your computer's mouse, drag each card into the first, second, or third position.

If you're asked the question about a troll wreaking havoc in the headmaster's study and which items you'd protect, place the items in the order you think appropriate. Click the Select This Order button to continue.

Some questions might give you a handful of options and ask you to choose just one. Here's an example:

> During your years studying at Hogwarts, you will learn many different lessons and skills. Which classes are you most excited to take? What magical skills are you looking forward to learning?

> Your choices are as follows:
> - Apparition and Disapparition
> - Transfiguration
> - Flying on a Broomstick
> - Hexes and Jinxes
> - All About Magical Creatures and How to Befriend/Care for Them
> - Secrets About the Castle
> - Every Area of Magic

Click the Select This Option button for the skill you most want to learn. Then, click the Yes, Please Proceed button to lock in your answer.

Wizarding Tip

For several of the questions the Sorting Hat might ask, you might simply be asked to choose between two options. Which you select is a matter of personal preference. Again, there is no right or wrong answer.

SCENE 3: THE SORTING HAT

The Sorting Hat now announces which of the four houses you'll be placed in! The decision is based on how you answered the questions. When your house name is revealed, click the Read Your Welcome Message button to learn more about your house.

Wizarding Tip

From this point forward, you can earn house points for your house. The house with the most points at the end of the school year wins the Pottermore House Cup. At anytime, click the Great Hall icon on the gateway to see which house is currently ahead.

Take a look at the top of the Pottermore screen. The gateway has once again changed. Now, when you look at the gateway, the Common Room and Great Hall icons have now been unlocked. When you click one of these icons, you can revisit these locations within Hogwarts at anytime during your adventure.

Notice that the Shield icon for your profile page (displayed just below the Pottermore title) now displays your house's insignia. Plus, to the left, just below the gateway, the number of house points you've personally earned is displayed.

Look to the right to see the total number of house points your house has earned thus far. Now, only one gateway icon remains locked. What this mysterious icon unlocks is revealed soon!

CHAPTER 8: THE POTIONS MASTER

Now that you're a Hogwarts student, it's time to get to work and begin your studies. It's an interesting time to be a student at Hogwarts. After all, Harry Potter is attending the school for the first time, and you're one of his classmates. To continue, click the right-arrow icon at the bottom of the screen next to the banner that says "The Sorting Hat" to access the Chapter 7 summary page.

Click the right arrow again to view the Chapter 8 chapter introduction page. You discover that Chapter 8, "The Potions Master," has three separate scenes. To enter into the first scene, click the Explore Chapter 8 button.

SCENE 1: HARRY'S EARLY DAYS AT HOGWARTS

Just as Harry Potter did, you want to explore Hogwarts and try to learn about some of the mysteries that surround this massive and very old castle. Start exploring the staircase and hallway. As you find items from this point forward, you now also earn house points.

A Message from Your Owl

Before Scene 1 begins, a message announces that the Great Hall is now open. This means you can begin earning house points for the house you've been assigned to. To enter into the Great Hall and see how many house points your house has collected, click the Great Hall icon that's been unlocked at the top of the screen, within the gateway.

When you enter this scene, you find yourself at the top of a staircase.

When standing at the top of the stairs, zoom in once and be sure to pick up the galleon on the floor. It's located between the carpet and the banister.

Wizarding Tip

On the first step (after zooming in once), not too far from where you picked up the galleon, you encounter the Circe chocolate frog card. Be sure to pick it up and add it to your collection as well.

Zoom in again and look near the windowsill at the bottom of the staircase. Here, you find a book called *Hogwarts: A History*. Add it to your collection of items.

Next, wave your mouse over the knight's armor to make it move. Be sure to study the painting on the right carefully. You might see the person within the picture move or leave the magical canvas altogether.

SCENE 2: HARRY'S FIRST POTIONS LESSON

Learning how to mix potions is an important skill for every young wizard or witch. As you make your way through your adventure, you can practice your potion-mixing skills. For every potion you successfully create, you earn house points.

Wizarding Tip

Whenever you feel like mixing a potion, from this point forward, you can simply click the Potions icon within the gateway (at the top of the screen).

Right now, it's time to start brewing your very first potion. Your first lesson involves creating the Cure for Boils. Click the Practice Brewing Cure for Boils button to get started.

Whenever you set out to create and mix a potion, you need to look up the recipe within a potions book. On the left side of the book's page, you find a list of required ingredients. Meanwhile, on the right page of the book, you see the step-by-step directions for mixing that potion.

Potion mixing takes practice. If you don't follow the directions, or you mix in the wrong ingredients, who knows what could happen? Plus, you always have to work quickly.

Before you try mixing a potion, click the potions book to review the recipe.

Wizarding Tip

Not only is it necessary to mix all the right ingredients in the correct order, you also need to complete the potion within the designated time period.

Like the spell book says, for this practice potion, your first step involves adding six snake fangs to the mortar. Then, crush them into tiny pieces. Pour four measures of crushed fangs into the cauldron. Next, heat up the mixture to 250, and hold it there for 10 seconds. Give your wand a wave, and then let the brew sit.

Use your mouse to move the various ingredients into the mortar or cauldron. The mortar and pestle, which is used for crushing ingredients, is on the left. The cauldron (a large pot) is to the right of it.

Magical Warning

Just above the caldron is the hourglass. When it runs out, so does the time you have for mixing the potion, so work quickly.

A Message from Your Owl

You learn more about mixing potions later in *Pottermore Secrets and Mysteries Revealed*.

Below the cauldron are its heat controls. On the right, you see the potions book that contains your recipe. Your ingredients are sitting on the table, waiting to be mixed.

SCENE 3: HAGRID'S WOODEN HOUSE

It's time to visit Hagrid at his wooden house. It's located outside of the Hogwarts Castle, along the edge of the Forbidden Forest. By the way, Hogwarts students are not allowed to visit this area outside the castle without permission. Are you going to follow the rules, or do whatever is necessary to help out your good friend?

Hmm. Decision made! Before going inside, see what you can find outside of Hagrid's house.

Wizarding Tip

You stumble upon the Paracelsus chocolate frog card to the immediate right of the barrel, near Hagrid's front stoop. It's on the ground.

To the immediate left of the barrel, also on the ground, is the wolfsbane. Add it to your collection.

Next, on the window ledge to the right, wave your mouse around until you find the dried billywig stings. Click the Collect button to grab it.

On the front of the hut (to the extreme left, next to the window), you also discover dried nettles, which you should collect as well.

Zoom in toward the front door of the house, and then wave your mouse around. You discover both a Collect button and a Closer Look button. Click the Closer Look button to reveal a newspaper article about the break-in at Gringotts. What was being stored within the vault that was broken into? This is a mystery you need to solve a bit later.

Next, click the Collect icon to unlock the homemade rock cake and add it to your collection.

Zoom in to get a closer look at what's located near the front door to Hagrid's house.

Now that you've completed Chapter 8, it's a great time to check out the Great Hall and see how your house is doing compared to the others. To do this, click the Great Hall icon within the gateway at the top of the screen. Then, to return to the Chapter 8 summary page, click the right-arrow icon that's located next to "The Potion Master" banner (near the bottom center of the screen).

CHAPTER 9: THE MIDNIGHT DUEL

When Harry Potter first got to Hogwarts, he made some really great friends, including Ron. However, there were some classmates, like Draco Malfoy, that he just didn't get along with.

From the Chapter 9 introduction page, click the Explore Chapter 9 button so that you can continue on in your adventure.

SCENE 1: FLYING LESSON

It's time for Harry to learn how to fly on a broomstick. This is an important skill for all Quidditch players to have, not to mention a quick way for all witches and wizards to travel around.

It's time to attend a Quidditch game.

Start by waving your mouse over Hermione's book bag. (She's the student in the middle.) You discover a hidden book, called *Quidditch Through the Ages*.

Now, zoom in two times to get a better look at Harry. He's riding his broomstick (in the sky). Click the object in front of him. You discover a remembrall. Grab it! If you wave your mouse over the Objects icon on the left side of the screen (under the Read About sign), a listing for the remembrall is now featured.

You're ready to move on to Scene 2 by clicking the right-arrow icon to the right of the "Flying Lesson" banner near the bottom center of the screen.

SCENE 2: THE TROPHY ROOM

The Hogwarts Castle is filled with large rooms that are full of old and interesting, often magical objects. The Trophy Room is no exception.

You definitely want to spend a few minutes exploring this room to find some useful items.

Look carefully on the trophy shelf to the immediate left of the doorway. Hidden on the third shelf from the bottom is the Salazar Slytherin chocolate frog card.

Zoom in once to view the doorway that leads to a hallway. Wave your mouse over the second suit of armor's head. The helmet opens, and inside is another shiny galleon for you to collect.

Zoom in a second time after grabbing the galleon. On the floor is an item. Upon closer inspection, it appears to be a jar of eels' eyes. Click the jar to collect it. The eels' eyes come in handy when mixing potions, so add them to your trunk.

Wizarding Tip

After grabbing the jar of eels' eyes, look down near the feet of the first body of armor that's closest to you in the hallway. Lurking in the shadows is Mrs. Norris (a cat). Wave your mouse over the creature and click the Read About button.

You'll discover and unlock familiars. These are animal-shaped spirits that serve witches in various ways. You can now read all about them by clicking the New from J.K. Rowling button. Plus, the entry for Familiars are included when you wave your mouse over the Creatures icon on the left side of the screen.

SCENE 3: THE FORBIDDEN CORRIDOR

Some places within Hogwarts Castle are very dangerous, and students are simply not allowed to enter these. As we all know, young Harry is very brave, as well as curious, so when he needs to accomplish something, he doesn't always follow the rules.

To continue exploring Hogwarts, it's now necessary to cast a spell to open a locked door. In this case, the spell you need to conjure up is called ALOHOMORA. Like potion mixing, spell casting is an essential skill that every Hogwarts student must learn and continuously practice.

A Message from Your Owl

By clicking the Spells icon within the gateway at the top of the screen, you can practice spell casting at anytime.

It's time to try casting your first spell. To do this, press the first letter of the spell using your mouse or the keyboard. You then notice a circle around each letter that starts to get brighter. When it's at its brightest, press or click the letter again. Watch as the magic flame proceeds to the next letter, and press it at the proper moment. When the circle is at its brightest point, click again. Timing is absolutely essential for proper spell casting.

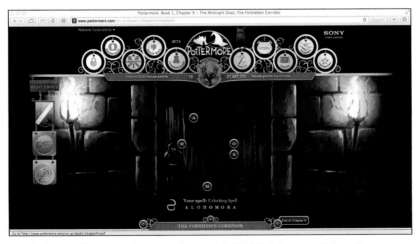

The Unlocking spell includes the letters A-L-O-H-O-M-O-R-A, but not all the letters are used. Notice the letters that are highlighted near the bottom of the screen, where it says "Your Spell."

To cast this particular spell, click the A that's above the lock to get started. When the circle around it is at its brightest, the press the A key again.

Now, follow the moving flame to the O, and when the flame touches it, press the O key. Press it again when the circle reaches its brightest point.

Then, follow the moving flame to the H. Repeat the previous steps again for the H, M, and the second A.

Wizarding Tip

For this spell, only the letters *A-O-H-M-A* are used, in that order.

If you get the timing right, the door magically unlocks and opens. This means you've mastered the ALOHOMORA spell.

However, if you didn't get the timing just right, or you pressed the wrong key at the wrong time, the spell doesn't work properly, and you need to try again.

After unlocking and opening the door, click the entranceway to walk inside. You're about to discover why this room was locked.

Can you hear a strange sound coming from ahead of you in the darkness? Zoom in twice. Yikes! Harry has discovered where the item from vault 713 that's missing from Gringotts is now being stored. You read about this theft earlier, in the newspaper article you found outside of Hagrid's house. This item is currently being very well protected by a monstrously large three-headed dog.

Click the right arrow next to "The Forbidden Corridor" banner to proceed to the Chapter 9 summary page. Then, click the right-arrow icon again to view the Chapter 10 introduction page. Click the Explore Chapter 10 button to continue.

CHAPTER 10: HALLOWEEN

Life at Hogwarts goes on for Harry. Each day is filled with new lessons and new adventures. But holidays, especially Halloween, are always a special time for Hogwarts students.

SCENE 1: HARRY'S SPECIAL DELIVERY

Someone has sent Harry a special gift: a new broomstick. Right now, it's on his bed within his dormitory.

Start by zooming in twice so that you can get a peak inside Harry's dorm room. Sitting next to the brand new Nimbus Two Thousand broomstick is a letter from Professor McGonagall. Click it to take a closer look.

As you discover, Harry is instructed to be at the Quidditch field at 7 p.m. for a special training session.

Wizarding Tip

Zoom all the way into the dorm room, and then wave your mouse over the lamp on the dresser to turn it on and off. Next, wave the mouse over the dresser drawers to make them open and close. Inside the bottom drawer, you discover a galleon. It pops out and lands on the floor. Pick it up.

SCENE 2: CHARM CLASS

Pay attention! Professor Flitwick is about to teach the class how to make objects levitate and fly around.

There's a lot more to do during this class than just listen to the professor speak.

Wave your mouse around to make a quill float into the air. Ugh. The quill quickly bursts into flames. Looks like you need more practice.

From the back of the classroom where you're sitting, zoom in just once. Look on the right side of the screen. Sitting on another student's desk is a galleon. Grab it.

The more galleons you collect, the more items you can buy later during visits to the shops along Diagon Alley.

Zoom in again and then click the chalkboard on the right side of the screen. Here, you unlock Hogwarts school subjects. Click the New from J.K. Rowling button to read more about it.

A Message from Your Owl

A listing for Hogwarts school subjects also appear on the left side of the screen, under the Places heading.

SCENE 3: THE MOUNTAIN TROLL

The bathroom within Hogwarts seems to have sprung a leak. Is it faulty plumbing, or is there something more sinister behind this flood?

You're about to discover that the cause of the plumbing problems is a 12-foot tall mountain troll who's not too happy.

Lying on the floor in the bathroom is a jar. Take a closer look at what's inside, then pick up the jar. Nice work. You just found some bat spleens. They are awesome ingredients to use in potions.

Wizarding Tip

Zoom in once and wave your mouse over the sink faucet to turn it off or back on.

After zooming in once, look on the wall, just past the last sink. You see a slug climbing up the wall. Collect it. It's a horned slug. These ugly little creatures are also used in potions as a cure for boils. Collect it.

Now zoom in again (as far as you can). This time, look around near the jack-o-lantern. Sitting on the ledge to the right of the jack-o-lantern is the Hengist of Woodcroft chocolate frog card. Be sure to collect it. It's hidden by the shadow cast by the troll, so look carefully. There are now only five more chocolate frog cards to find and collect, so keep looking.

Your Attention Please...

If you're following along in the *Harry Potter and the Sorcerer's Stone* book, you know that it was during this wet incident when Harry and Ron discovered the troll that they also become friends with Hermione Granger. The three of them managed to knock out the troll, without getting hurt themselves. What evolves into a lifelong friendship between our heroes, Harry, Hermione, and Ron, has begun!

CHAPTER 11: QUIDDITCH

As fall and winter roll around, the temperature outside drops. Harry Potter and the other students at Hogwarts continue their studies. Just like in any school, being a student at Hogwarts requires a lot of hard work, including hour after hour of studying, and participating in countless classes and lectures.

However, Hogwarts students are allowed to have some fun, too. For example, the most popular sport at the school is Quidditch, and young Harry has discovered that he's an awesome player.

SCENE 1: CHARMS HOMEWORK

The Gryffindor common room is where Harry, Ron, Hermione, and the rest of the Gryffindor gang often gather to do their homework and study. As you enter into the room, check out what's on the table in front of you.

Wizarding Tip

Click the open book near the center of the table. You discover the original forty. A listing for the original forty unlocks and appears under the Characters heading on the left side of the screen.

From this newly unlocked information, you get a true behind-the-scenes look at J.K. Rowling's original thoughts and notes from when she was creating the Harry Potter series. After you read this information, when you wave your mouse over the book, the pages magically turn.

Here's how the Gryffindor common room looks when you first enter.

You have another chance to increase your bank account in this scene. Look to the left of the glowing blue jar on the window sill. You discover a galleon that you can collect.

Wizarding Tip

Zoom in on the glowing jar on the windowsill. It contains Hermione's blue fire. Wave your mouse over the jar and the glow turns on or off. While you're looking at the jar, if you zoom in a second time, you get a good view of Hagrid's house through the window.

SCENE 2: THE GOLDEN SNITCH

Young witches and wizards at Hogwarts love to play Quidditch. In fact, the competition between the four houses gets rather intense when it comes to winning the Quidditch Cup.

In this game, the objective is to catch the golden snitch, but it's a very difficult task that's left to only the most highly skilled players.

Zoom in twice and try to catch the golden snitch. First, get the snitch in focus. Then, try to click it. Be quick!

Wizarding Tip

To catch the golden snitch, study its flight pattern. It follows a somewhat-predictable triangular path. Instead of trying to chase it with your mouse, wait for it to stop at one location, and then click it. After you've grabbed the golden snitch, click the Collect button and add it to your trunk.

The main objective in this scene is to help Harry catch the snitch.

Wizarding Tip

Can you spot Hermione in the crowd below? She's the one with the blue flame. After grabbing the snitch (while still zoomed in twice), look for the glowing blue jar she's holding. When you wave the mouse over it, the glow intensifies.

CHAPTER 12: THE MIRROR OF ERISED

The Christmas season has arrived at Hogwarts and everyone is in a festive mood. It might be snowing outside, but it's toasty warm inside the library, where the next scene takes place.

SCENE 1: THE LIBRARY

Looking from left to right within the library, you see four bookshelves that are stacked from floor to ceiling with all sorts of fascinating books about magic, potions, and other enchanted topics.

You discover some important books here in the library.

Without zooming in, wave the mouse over the second bookshelf from the left. About halfway up on the shelf, you discover a book called *A Study of Recent Developments in Wizardry*. Collect it.

Also while exploring the library, you want to locate and collect another book, called *Important Modern Magical Discoveries*. It's located in the same general area as *A Study of Recent Developments in Wizardry*.

Now, zoom in and take a look at the third shelf from the left. Look around here for a third book, called *Notable Magical Names of Our Time*. It's another great volume to add to your collection.

Finally, be sure to locate the book *Great Wizards of the Twentieth Century* before leaving the library. It now looks like you have some reading to do with all the new books that you've discovered in the library.

Wizarding Tip

From the point when you first enter the library, zoom in twice on the last bookshelf from the left. Look toward the bottom, you find the Merlin chocolate frog card. It's hidden between some books.

SCENE 2: CHRISTMAS AT HOGWARTS

One of the wonderful things about Pottermore is that you can share your adventure with other online friends. In the spirit of Christmas, you can send any of your online friends gifts. To do this, click the Friends icon within the gateway at the top of the screen.

As you partake in this holiday feast, navigate your way around the floating candles, scrumptious food, and the multitude of presents to see what you can discover and collect.

A Message from Your Owl

It's in this chapter of *Harry Potter and the Sorcerer's Stone* that Harry receives his invisibility cloak as a very special Christmas gift. He later uses this cloak to explore Hogwarts without being detected.

The holiday season is a time to celebrate.

On the bench right in front of you, click the book *Curses and Counter Curses* and add it to your collection. Then zoom in a bit, just above where you found the book and collect a galleon.

Wizarding Tip

Zoom in once and wave your mouse over the pink colored party favors that are on the table in front of you. You see a few adorable white mice scampering around. Also, look for the green and white party favor that's sitting on the corner of the table that's closest to you. Click it to make it levitate and explode. Surprise! You're given a brand new chess set that you can now collect.

Also, after zooming one once, be sure to click the green jar on the left side of the table. It contains infusion of wormwood. This is another powerful ingredient that can be used when mixing potions. A golden galleon is also now visible and can be collected.

Wizarding Tip

From the point where you first entered the scene, zoom in twice (as close as you can on the table). Wave your mouse over the balloon. Watch as it floats into the air and then pops. Then, to the right of where you found the balloon, in between the two trees, look between the floating candles to find and collect mistletoe berries.

SCENE 3: THE DISUSED CLASSROOM

When Harry walks into this dark room, he figures it's just an old classroom that's no longer used for anything but storage. Can you see the chairs and desks piled up in the left corner?

Zoom in twice, and then click the Mirror of Erised. You can read some new information about this enchanted object as soon as the Read About button appears and you click it.

Notice that the entry for the Mirror of Erised is now unlocked and accessible from within the Objects box on the left side of the screen.

Directly in front of Harry is the old and very large Mirror of Erised.

A Message from Your Owl

What could the Mirror of Erised possibly be used for? The only clue is the inscription on it: Erised stra ehru oyt ube cafru oyt on wohsi.

Wizarding Tip

While zoomed in on the mirror, search around to the immediate right of Harry. You find another galleon.

CHAPTER 13: NICOLAS FLAMEL

What Harry saw in the Mirror of Erised confused him a bit. However, Professor Dumbledore convinced the young wizard not to return to the mirror—at least for a while. After the Christmas break, Harry becomes busier than ever with his studies and Quidditch practice.

After one particularly tiring practice, Harry goes back to the Gryffindor common room to meet up with Ron and Hermione.

SCENE 1: NICOLAS FLAMEL IS FINALLY REVEALED

This lovely room is filled with interesting items. As you stay warm in front of the crackling fire, take a look around. See what you uncover.

Start by waving your mouse over the chessboard to move pieces around. When you wave the mouse over the candle next to the chessboard, it blows out, but with another wave, you can relight it.

A Message from Your Owl

Did you know that Nicholas Flamel was an alchemist and the maker of the Sorcerer's Stone? This object is believed to hold amazing powers.

While in this room, you learn a bit more about Nicholas Flamel and perhaps about the infamous and much-needed Sorcerer's Stone as well.

Now, zoom in and take a closer look at the open book that's sitting on the chair to the right. Read a bit about the study of alchemy from the pop-up window that appears on the screen. Next, click the right side of the book to unlock information about Nicolas Flamel.

A Message from Your Owl

When you unlock the information about Nicolas Flamel, click the New from J.K. Rowling button. Plus, details about him appear under the Characters heading on the left side of the screen. According to J.K. Rowling, Nicolas Flamel was a real-life person. He was a businessman and philanthropist from Paris.

Wizarding Tip

If you look closely on the table near the chess set, there appears to be a chocolate frog card sitting on the table. However, this particular card is not collectible, so just leave it where it is.

SCENE 2: THE HOODED FIGURE

This scene takes place outside, near the edge of the Forbidden Forest. Once again, some exploration is needed to discover what's hidden here.

There's probably a good reason why Hogwarts students aren't allowed to explore the Forbidden Forest. But, Harry is brave and on a mission, so nothing is going to stop him.

Start by waving your mouse over the large tree on the left to make its branches move. Then, on the ground, almost directly in front of where you're standing (in front of some bushes that are to the left of the greenhouse), you find another galleon. Collect it.

Also on the ground in front of you, even closer to you than the galleon's location, you discover the Helga Hufflepuff chocolate frog card. It's very difficult to spot, so slowly move your mouse around until you stumble upon it. Grab the card for your collection.

CHAPTER 14: NORBERT THE NORWEGIAN RIDGEBACK

Here in Chapter 14, there are three scenes to explore, starting with "Hagrid's Secret," which takes place in the Hogwarts library.

Wizarding Tip

Remember, you can leave Pottermore.com at anytime and return to your adventure. Pick up exactly where you left off by entering through the magical gateway. Just click the book and chapter number you want to return to. In this case, click Chapter 14 of *Harry Potter and the Sorcerer's Stone*.

SCENE 1: HAGRID'S SECRET

This scene takes place in a different section of the library. Harry and his friends again find themselves surrounded by old books. These volumes contain knowledge obtained by thousands of witches and wizards who came before them.

Once again, the search is on for a few important books. Along with Harry and his friends, someone else is lurking in the shadows and secretly searching for books. By the size of the shadow being cast, it can only be Hagrid.

Harry wants to help out his friend Hagrid, but to do this, he needs to learn more about whatever it is that Hagrid is researching.

Pass your mouse over the light on the desk to turn it on and brighten up the room.

Wizarding Tip

Wave your mouse over the open book on the desk to make the pages turn.

Be sure to zoom in once on the bookshelf that's to the left of the doorway. On the second shelf from the bottom, there's a book to collect. It's *From Egg to Inferno, A Dragon Keeper's Guide*. This could be useful to Hagrid who just so happens to be raising a dragon.

You discover another book that needs to be collected to the left of Ron, on the second shelf from the bottom. This one is called *Dragon Species of Great Britain and Ireland*.

To find some of the books in the library, you have to zoom in.

Directly below that book, there's another one called *Modern Magical History* that also needs to be picked up.

SCENE 2: THE EGG IN THE FIRE

Back at Hagrid's house, something is warming up in the fireplace. No, this isn't Hagrid's next meal, and it doesn't look like an ordinary egg.

Harry is determined to figure out what Hagrid is hiding. You can discover some clues within his house.

Wizarding Tip

Check out the table on the right. Click the book. It's called *Dragon Breeding for Pleasure and Profit*. Add it to your collection. You can also wave your mouse over nearby objects to make them move.

Zoom in twice. When you pass your mouse over the kettle, steam comes out of its spout. Or, when you wave your mouse over the cooking utensils hanging by the fireplace, they move slightly, and you hear the screeching sound of metal.

Now, click the giant egg surrounded by flames. Just as you suspected, it's a dragon egg. Collect it.

SCENE 3: A PLAN FOR NORBERT THE BABY DRAGON

Having a pet is a wonderful experience. Muggles love dogs, cats, and hamsters. Wizards also like cats, but sometimes prefer owls or toads to be their magical companions.

Hagrid, however, has a pet dragon. He's named it Norbert. The problem with dragons is that they're cute when they're babies, but they grow up to be very large… and they breathe fire!

Harry and Hermione agree to help give Norbert away when Hagrid can no longer care for the fast-growing creature in secret. But, Harry and Hermione can't get caught wondering around the halls of Hogwarts at night. Lucky for Harry, he has his invisibility cloak to keep them hidden.

Harry and Hermione come up with a plan about what to do with Norbert.

Wizarding Tip

On the roof of this castle tower, wave your mouse over the wooden box in the center. Can you hear Norbert trying to escape?

Move your mouse slightly to the left. What's that glimmering next to the carton? It's Harry's invisibility cloak.

Now, take a look to the left near the door. Pick up the galleon that's on the floor. When you wave your mouse over the doorway, it opens and closes. As you can see, it's late at night. In fact, it's around midnight on a Saturday.

Zoom in twice and look up into the sky, to the right of Harry and Hermione. Can you see Charlie's four friends flying in on broomsticks. They're coming to pick up Norbert.

Harry and Hermione are so relieved to hand Norbert over to Charlie's friends that they accidentally left the invisibility cloak outside on the roof of the castle tower. That means they could easily be spotted roaming around Hogwarts at night. Getting caught means detention!

CHAPTER 15: THE FORBIDDEN FOREST

Harry and Hermione now have to face Professor McGonagall and explain what they were doing roaming around Hogwarts alone late at night. If they tell the truth about helping Hagrid give away his pet dragon, it will get them into even more trouble, because dragons are not allowed to be kept as pets at Hogwarts.

SCENE 1: HARRY BECOMES AN OUTCAST

Back in the library once again, there are a handful of items to collect and several things to discover.

Collect some books and make other books levitate while you're visiting the library this time.

First, wave your mouse over the open book directly in front of you. This makes the pages magically turn.

To the right of the book, also on the desk, you discover a galleon. Pick it up. If you don't see the galleon right away, wave your mouse over the desk lamp to turn it on. When the room is brighter, you easily spot the galleon.

It's now time to test your magical powers for making objects levitate. Wave your mouse near the top of the bookshelves on the left. This causes books to fly off the shelf from each side of the library, spin around, and then switch places.

Zoom in once and see whether you can find any additional books that are worthy of collecting. You discover *A Beginner's Guide to Transfiguration* on the second set of bookcases on the left. This is a difficult one to spot, so wave your mouse slowly around the area until the Read About button appears.

Wizarding Tip

When you zoom in twice (as far as you can), you can also turn on the lamp on the desk in the back of the library.

Zoom in toward the stained glass window in the back of the library. Near the windowsill, you discover the book *One Thousand Magical Herbs and Fungi*. Click the New from J.K. Rowling button to read a short but informative excerpt from the book.

On the windowsill to the left, you find the Rowena Ravenclaw chocolate frog card. Add it to your collection.

While still zoomed in twice, look at the very top shelf on the left (near the ceiling) for a book called *The Dark Forces: A Guide to Self-Protection*. Again, when you click the New from J.K. Rowling button, you're able to read a portion of this book.

SCENE 2: INTO THE FORBIDDEN FOREST

It's a dark night. The perfect time for Harry to experience another exciting adventure. He's off to explore the Forbidden Forest.

To the immediate left when you enter the Forbidden Forest, click the mushroom that's growing on the ground. It's a leaping toadstool—another powerful ingredient that can be used in potions.

Wizarding Tip

Wave your mouse over the birds perched in the trees to make them fly away. Then, near the base of the tree on the right, you can see spiders moving around. If you look closely, you also see the glowing eyes of other tiny creatures who are hiding within the tree.

Zoom in once and pick up the wolfsbane that's also on the ground, a bit to the left of where you're standing.

Something or someone evil is lurking within the Forbidden Forest. Shown here is the wolfsbane after zooming in once. Click the Collect button to grab it.

Now, while you're still zoomed in once, move to the right, just a tad, and pick up the bright silver object lying on the ground. It's unicorn blood. This is an incredible find!

Unicorn blood can be used to keep someone alive who is very close to death. However, it's a very serious crime if you harm a unicorn.

Finding unicorn blood in the forest can mean just one thing: A unicorn has been injured or killed. Who would possibly do such a thing? Only one evil person comes to mind!

Zoom in as far as you can (twice) and look to the right. What you see is none other than Lord Voldemort. He's leaning over the magical creature stealing its blood. This is some of the dark magic that You-Know-Who is using to stay alive.

CHAPTER 16: THROUGH THE TRAPDOOR

Lord Voldemort is making his evil plans to return. Only one young wizard, with the help of his loyal friends, has the power to stop him. Harry Potter might be young and inexperienced as a wizard, but he's brave and has vast magical powers that not even he truly understands yet.

SCENE 1: THE WINGED KEYS

Harry finds himself in a room with a locked door. Winged keys are flying around everywhere. However, only one key opens the door he must pass through. Your objective is to find the correct key.

Wizarding Tip

The easiest way to find the winged key you're looking for is to wave your mouse around slowly until the Collect button appears.

Harry comes face to face with hundreds, maybe thousands, of colorful winged keys. Click as many fast-moving keys as you can until you find the right one.

When you find the correct key, you can collect it and add it to your trunk. After you have the key, click the right arrow next to "The Winged Keys" banner at the bottom of the screen to move on to Scene 2.

SCENE 2: THE CHESSBOARD CHAMBER

What you discover within this room is a giant chessboard. Unfortunately, you don't have time for a game right now. Instead, you need to discover a way out of the room through a door located just past the king and queen chess pieces.

Wave your mouse around on the right side of the screen to move one of the knights and turn on some lights.

Wizarding Tip

Zoom in twice and wave your mouse between the king and queen chess pieces to light up the room.

SCENE 3: THE POTION PUZZLE

Throughout his time at Hogwarts, Harry experiences many challenges. Here, you must choose the correct potions to solve a puzzle. To learn more, click the scroll that's sitting on the right side of the desk.

Go ahead, take a closer look at the scroll. It seems that danger lies ahead, while safety is behind you. The scroll reveals clues about which potions to select.

Wizarding Tip

Based on what you learn from the scroll, click the smallest blue bottle first. It's the one that's third from the left.

Choose the right potion bottles to solve the puzzle.

Wizarding Tip

After you select the first correct potion, you still need to choose the second. You have six possible options. Based on the clues you read within the scroll, click the purple potion bottle on the right to solve this puzzle.

After solving this puzzle, click the right arrow at the bottom of the screen next to "The Potion Puzzle" banner. You're ready to move on to Chapter 17.

CHAPTER 17: THE MAN WITH TWO FACES

The adventures Harry Potter experiences within *Harry Potter and the Sorcerer's Stone* are coming to an end. However, as we all know, so much more lies ahead for him as his battle against Lord Voldemort escalates!

The final chapter of this book within Pottermore still awaits. Your immediate goal is to find the Sorcerer's Stone and confront You-Know-Who. This ultimately enables you to unlock more of the magical gateway within Pottermore and continue your adventure.

SCENE 1: THE SORCERER'S STONE

"The final chapter awaits…" is the message you'll see displayed on the screen before you enter into the first scene of Chapter 17. It's time to find and unlock the Sorcerer's Stone.

A shadowy figure in a robe stands before you. It's Professor Quirrel.

Harry is standing the closest to you. Wave your mouse around his robe, near his hand. What's that sitting in his pocket? Click the Read About button to find out. You've found the Sorcerer's Stone.

Wizarding Tip

If you haven't already done so, be sure to read the exclusive new information about the Sorcerer's Stone. After locating and unlocking it, you can do this by clicking the New from J.K. Rowling button, or by clicking the Sorcerer's Stone listing under the Objects heading on the left side of the screen.

Now zoom in once and click Professor Quirrel's face. He's the shadowy figure who is facing Harry. You unlock Quirinus Quirrell and are able to learn more about him by clicking the New from J.K. Rowling button.

Harry has done it! He's found and unlocked the Sorcerer's Stone and, at least temporarily, slowed down the evil plans of You-Know-Who.

SCENE 2: THE HOSPITAL WING

Luckily, Harry survived his first major encounter with Lord Voldemort. He now finds himself recuperating within the infirmary at Hogwarts.

There's not much for Harry to do here but to relax and recover from his ordeal. When you explore the infirmary room, you find a few things to collect.

Start by finding and grabbing the chocolate frog card sitting on the leftmost chair. Zoom in once to find it. It's the Cliodna chocolate frog card.

Zoom in again and look for the bottle that's on the shelf next to the bathroom door. When you collect it, you discover it's filled with salamander blood. This is the perfect ingredient to increase the power of certain potions.

In the infirmary, you need to zoom in twice to collect the bottle on the shelf and obtain the salamander blood.

Also, while zoomed in twice, be sure to search the medicine cabinet near the back wall. You come across a bezoar. It's a stone that comes from the stomach of a goat. It's used to protect wizards and witches from some poisons.

SCENE 3: THE END-OF-YEAR FEAST

What an extraordinary year it's been at Hogwarts—not just for Harry but for all the students (and the faculty, too).

Yes, Lord Voldemort has returned (at least he's trying to). But, for the moment, everyone is safe. It's the perfect time for a celebration!

Wizarding Tip

Click near the center of the professor's table to discover the Godric Gryffindor chocolate frog card. It's between Professor McGonagall's cup and Professor Dumbledore's podium.

There's also a galleon on the floor that you can pick up. It's directly in front of Professor Dumbledore.

Wizarding Tip

Wave your mouse across the colorful banners on the wall. Magically, a video window featuring J.K. Rowling appears.

It's the end-of-year feast at Hogwarts. Everyone deserves to celebrate!

A Message from Your Owl

In this final scene, you can't zoom in. But you can move slightly left or right as you enjoy the festivities.

One riveting Harry Potter adventure has come to an end. However, another is a about to begin.

In the months and years to come, Pottermore.com will be your portal to experience many more interactive adventures that re-create memorable scenes from the bestselling books in the Harry Potter series.

Up next, of course, is *Harry Potter and the Chamber of Secrets*.

A Message from Your Owl

You've now made it through Book 1 within Pottermore. But, you can still return often to re-read the exclusive information offered by J.K. Rowling. Plus, you can share your thoughts and ideas about your favorite moments by posting comments or your own artwork.

Of course, you can also continue earning house points for your particular house by casting spells or mixing potions, while also exchanging gifts and interacting with your fellow Harry Potter fans.

To do this, click the Spells or Potions icon within the gateway at the top of the screen. By experiencing these other elements of Pottermore, you can break away from Harry's adventure and experience more of your own magical moments!

Wizarding Tip

Since Pottermore.com first went online, a few new items have been added throughout Book 1 that you can collect. Go back and see what you can find.

Now is a good time to click the Trunk icon within the gateway at the top of the screen. As you're looking at the Trunk page, click the Chocolate Frog Cards button to see your collection. By now, you should have all 11 of the cards. Also within your trunk should be 15 books and 21 objects.

Wizarding Tip

Before moving forward onto Book 2, consider clicking your profile. Review all of your character's accomplishments. How many house points have you personally earned so far? How many spell books do you have, and how many spells have you cast? Have you started mixing potions yet? There's still so much more to experience within Pottermore.

IV

WIZARD'S DUELS: ENHANCE YOUR SPELL-CASTING SKILLS

During your Pottermore adventure through Book I, *Harry Potter and the Sorcerer's Stone*, you made your way to Chapter 9, "The Midnight Duel." After playing a game of Quidditch and then visiting the Trophy Room, in Scene 3, "The Forbidden Corridor," you had to use your magic wand and cast your first spell.

Casting spells is a definite part of the main Pottermore adventure, but another aspect of Pottermore allows you to practice casting many different types of spells. You can challenge either your fellow housemates or witches or wizards from different houses to a Wizard's Duel.

A Message from Your Owl

When you practice casting spells yourself, or when you challenge people from your own house to a Wizard's Duel, you don't earn any house points when you successfully cast a spell or win a practice duel. The only way to earn house points for yourself and your house is to challenge Pottermore players from other houses to a Wizard's Duel…and win!

Spell casting is a skill that every witch and wizard must master. During your time as a student at Hogwarts School of Witchcraft and Wizardry, you take numerous classes that cover all aspects of spell casting. However, casting spells also takes practice and skill.

To hone your skills and practice casting spells, click the Spells icon within the gateway. After this icon is unlocked, you can practice your spell casting or participate in Wizard's Duels at anytime.

A BEGINNER'S GUIDE TO SPELL CASTING

Displayed near the top-right corner of the Spells screen (after you click the Spells icon within the gateway), you see how many spells you've already discovered. You can find these spells within the spell books along the left side of the screen.

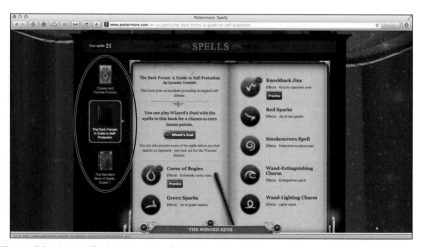

The spell books you find or purchase from the shops in Diagon Alley help you practice casting spells and serve you well during Wizard's Duels.

Depending on when you access the Spells area of Pottermore, some of the spell books at your disposal might include *Curses and Counter-Curses*, *The Dark Forces: A Guide to Self-Protection*, and *The Standard Book of Spells, Grade 1*.

Each book contains a separate selection of spells you can practice casting or actually use in a Wizard's Duel.

Wizarding Tip

As you browse through your spell books, only some of them display Practice buttons. When you click a Practice button, you can practice casting that particular spell on your own. For those spells that don't have a Practice button, you need to unlock and discover how to use them later, as you progress further into Pottermore.

Keep in mind that some spells from spell books that are displayed early on in your adventure might not become available to you until much later, even after you've completed Book 1.

HOW TO CAST A SPELL

Before you start dueling others, take some time to practice spell casting on your own. One at a time, select a spell to practice by clicking the Practice button below the spell.

As you discover, spell casting in Pottermore is all about timing and quick reflexes. When you're about to cast a spell, the name of the spell and the magic words that go along with it appear near the bottom center of the screen.

Notice that when you look at the magic words that some of the letters are highlighted. For example, if you click the Practice button for the Full Body Bind spell, the magic words to cast this spell are *Petrificus Totalus*. However, only the letters *P*, *T*, *F*, *C*, *T*, *L*, and *S* are highlighted.

The special symbol to the left of the magic words help you anticipate where to click next if you're using a mouse or trackpad to cast spells, as opposed to pressing letter keys on the keyboard.

This is what the screen looks like when you're about to cast the Full Body Bind spell.

These are the letters you need to press on your keyboard, in order, after the spell-casting process begins. As soon as you press the letter *P*, a white circle appears around the letter. The circle quickly grows and then shrinks. Instead of pressing the actual letter keys, you can also use your mouse or trackpad to click the letters displayed on the screen (in the correct order and at exactly the right moment, of course).

When the circle is at its largest size, press the *P* key on your keyboard again. Perfect timing is absolutely essential. The moving white flame quickly proceeds toward the next letter (in this case, the *T*). As soon as the flame touches the *T*, press the *T* key.

Wizarding Tip

You have greater success casting spells if you wait until the circle is at its largest size around a letter before pressing that letter a second time.

A growing white circle now surrounds the letter *T*. Again, when the circle is at its largest point, press the *T* key a second time to make the fire jump to the next letter. Keep repeating this process until you've completed all the letters in the sequence that make up the spell.

Watch the moving white flame closely as it quickly travels from letter to letter, and press the right key at the right moment.

In some cases, the letters on the screen are close together. This gives you a very short amount of time to react. Your best bet is to memorize the letter combination required for each spell, and then position your fingers on the keyboard accordingly so that you're ready to press the right keys, in the right order, at exactly the right moment.

Wizarding Tip

Try to memorize the letter combination required to cast the spells that are available to you. This helps to increase your speed and accuracy.

A Message from Your Owl

Instead of pressing the letter keys on the keyboard, you also have the option to click the letters using your mouse. Either way works, but both methods require perfect timing. Figure out which method is easiest for you and use it.

If you press a letter too soon or too late, the spell fails! Based on how accurately and quickly you complete a spell, you receive a Spell Cast Potency Score. The higher the score, the more potent the spell. Every spell has a different maximum score you can earn by executing it perfectly. Even if you don't cast the spell correctly, you are given a Spell Cast Potency Score (but it is very low).

Wizarding Tip

Your goal should be to earn a Spell Cast Potency Score of 140 or higher. This almost always guarantees a win (or at least a draw) when you participate in a Wizard's Duel against an opponent from another house.

Of course, you can get a lower score, but to win, you score needs to be higher than your opponent's score. The winner of a duel earns five house points.

As you work with the different spells, you discover that some generate higher Spell Cast Potency Scores than others. For example, the Full Body Bind and Tongue-Tying spell, if executed perfectly, generate higher scores than easier-to-cast spells.

A Message from Your Owl

If a spell you're casting fails during a practice session and you want to try it again immediately, wait for the score screen to display, and then click the Refresh icon within your web browser. The intro screen for that spell then reappears. Click the Cast Spell Now button to try again.

Otherwise, if from the score screen you press the Return to Spells button, you are returned to the main Spells screen. You then have to reselect the spell to try it again. Doing this requires extra steps.

YOU CAN CAST MANY DIFFERENT SPELLS

By the time you finish Book 1, *Harry Potter and the Sorcerer's Stone*, within Pottermore, you have acquired or learned at least 10 different spells that you can cast. From the Spells screen, start by clicking the spell book called *Curses and Counter-Curses*. You can find it along the left side of the Spells screen.

After you click the Curses and Counter-Curses *book cover, the spells you can cast from it are displayed.*

Wizarding Tip

Some spells require you to press the same letter twice in a row as part of the letter sequence. The Tickling Hex and Tongue-Tying spells are examples of this. These spells are a bit easier to cast because you have fewer letters to remember.

Magical Warning

Spells with letter sequences located close together on the screen are more challenging to cast because it takes even less time for the moving flame to travel between those letters. You have to react even faster to achieve success. The Jelly-Legs Curse is an example of a spell whose letter sequence is placed close together.

PARTICIPATING IN WIZARD'S DUELS

After you've spent some time practicing your spells, why not try an actual duel against another opponent? If you select someone to duel from your own house, it's considered practice, so you don't have to worry about your opponent winning house points if you lose.

Remember, earning house points can help your house compete successfully and maybe even win the Pottermore House Cup.

To participate in a Wizard's Duel, click the Spells icon within the gateway. Then, click the Wizard's Duel button. The Wizard's Duel screen appears. This screen has three sections.

Under the Your Duels heading, you can view duels you've recently participated in. You can also challenge a previous opponent to a rematch or accept a new challenge. Under the Challenge a Friend heading, you can pick one of your online friends and challenge that person to a duel. Or, you can find a random person from another house to challenge by clicking the emblem for another house under the Challenge a House heading.

From the Wizard's Duel screen, you can accept challenges from other people, initiative your own challenges, request a rematch, or view details about past duels.

A Message from Your Owl

If you click the emblem for another house from under the Choose a House heading of the Wizard's Duel screen, Pottermore matches you up with a random opponent. You don't discover who it is until you see the score screen after the duel. When you do this, the winner of the duel earns five house points. The loser gets nothing.

Wizarding Tip

You can practice against random opponents from your own house by clicking your house emblem under the Practice Against Your Own House heading. When you do this, you are matched up against someone else, but no house points are awarded to the winner.

Another way to initiate a Wizard's Duel with one of your Pottermore friends is to click the Friends icon from within the gateway. Then, as you're looking at your list of friends, click the Challenge button below one of them.

Before choosing someone to duel against from your Friends list, look for a green dot near the upper-left corner of their animal avatar. This indicates that someone is online and available for a duel. If you see a red dot, that person is not currently online. You can still initiate a Wizard's Duel, but you have to wait for that person to come back online to take her turn in the duel.

Also, pay attention to the other person's house. Remember, if you challenge someone from your own house, it's considered practice. But if you challenge someone from another house, the winner earns five house points.

A Message from Your Owl

During a Wizarding Duel, each witch or wizard can select and try casting just one spell. The person with the highest Spell Cast Potency Score wins that duel. The person who initiated the challenge goes first. Then, the challenger needs to wait for the opponent to try casting his spell before the results are displayed.

If the opponent isn't currently online, you need to wait for that person to return to Pottermore and accept your challenge before you can see the results. Immediately after a Wizard's Duel, if both people are online, click the Rematch button to challenge that same person again without having to wait.

HOW TO RESPOND TO WIZARD'S DUEL REQUESTS

If someone has sent you a duel request, you receive a notification. A Number icon near the Messenger Owl with either appear, or the number within the icon will increase. Click the Messenger Owl to view your notifications.

When you see a message under the Wizard's Duel heading that says "Your challenges awaiting:" followed by a number, click the Go to Wizard's Duel button to access the Wizard's Duels page.

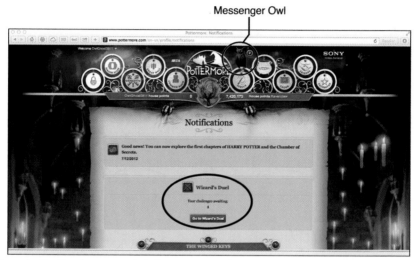

From the Notifications page, click the Go to Wizard's Duel button if you have been challenged to a Wizard's Duel.

When viewing the Wizard's Duel page, under the Your Duels heading you see the username of the person who has challenged you to a duel, as well as that person's house and when the challenge was issued. Click the Duel button to accept the duel request and engage in a Wizard's Duel against that challenger. You also have the option to click the Decline button if you don't want to duel that person.

UNLOCK MORE SPELLS AS YOUR ADVENTURE CONTINUES

The spells listed in this section are the ones available to you after you've completed Book 1, *Harry Potter and the Sorcerer's Stone*. However, as you progress further in Pottermore, you have the opportunity to discover and unlock additional spells that you can use during your adventure, when practicing your spells, or as you're engaged in Wizard's Duels.

Remember to keep practicing! Being able to successfully complete each spell is an important skill. However, you earn more Spell Cast Potency points by successfully casting each spell as quickly as possible.

POTION BREWING FOR HOGWARTS STUDENTS

You could say that potion mixing and brewing is a lot like baking. If you're in your kitchen at home and mix all the right ingredients to bake chocolate chip cookies from scratch, and then bake the cookie dough for just the right amount of time, the end result is something incredibly delicious.

But, if you forget an ingredient, use the wrong ingredients, don't bake the dough long enough, or you accidently leave the cookies in the oven for too long, what you wind up with is a yucky mess that nobody wants to eat. The same is true when it comes to brewing potions.

Like spell casting, potion brewing is a skill that all Hogwarts students absolutely must learn to do well. This is why one of the things you're required to bring with you to Hogwarts is your very own cauldron, which you buy at Potage's Cauldron Shop along Diagon Alley.

Beyond having to successfully brew specific potions to help you get through your Pottermore adventure, you can brew all sorts of potions at anytime after you've unlocked the Potions area of Pottermore. When this happens, you're able to click the Potions icon within the gateway.

In Pottermore, successfully brewing potions is one of the ways you can earn house points (and help your house work toward winning the Pottermore House Cup). But, if you fail to brew a potion correctly, instead of being awarded house points, you lose house points. Plus, you could accidently melt your cauldron, which means you'd need to purchase a replacement.

A SUCCESSFUL POTION STARTS WITH THE PERFECT CAULDRON

Depending on the potion you're trying to brew, you need to use a brass, copper, or pewter cauldron. Yes, in most cases, the type of cauldron you use is as important as the ingredients you put into it. This is why you need to follow the potion recipe from your potion books perfectly.

When you visit Potage's Cauldron Shop along Diagon Alley, you find all the different types of cauldrons available for sale.

In Book 1, Chapter 5, Scene 3, "Harry Goes Shopping," you have the opportunity to explore the shops along Diagon Alley and purchase all the items listed on the shopping list that came with your admission letter for Hogwarts School of Witchcraft and Wizardry.

At anytime after that, you can return to Diagon Alley by clicking the Diagon Alley icon within the gateway. As long as you have enough galleons, you can purchase any of the cauldrons and the ingredients you need to brew various potions.

A Message from Your Owl

It's also possible to receive a cauldron or potion ingredients as gifts from other people.

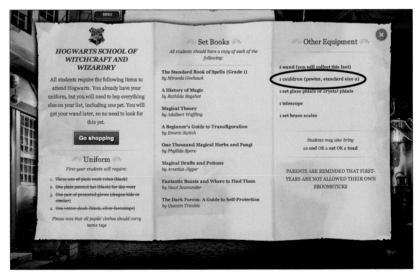

Your shopping list from Hogwarts requires you to buy a size 2 pewter cauldron. It's listed under Other Equipment. After you purchase the cauldron, it gets stored within your trunk and becomes available whenever you need it.

As you arrive at Diagon Alley, Potage's Cauldron Shop is the first store you see on the left. The shop's sign is shaped like a cauldron. Click the door to go inside. After inside the shop, you find the selection of cauldrons currently available on the shelf.

While you're experiencing Book 1 within Pottermore, you're able to buy a size 2 brass cauldron for 21 galleons, a size 2 copper cauldron for 25 galleons, or a size 2 pewter cauldron for 15 galleons.

Wizarding Tip

After you've purchased the type of cauldron you need, click the Potions icon within the gateway to begin brewing a potion. Or, while still visiting Diagon Alley, drop into the Apothecary (which is next door to Potage's Cauldron Shop, also on the left) to stock up on ingredients.

SHOP FOR POTION INGREDIENTS AT THE APOTHECARY

During your Pottermore adventure, you find and are able to collect a wide range of potion ingredients that you can later use to brew potions. However, from the Apothecary on Diagon Alley, you can shop for all the additional ingredients you need, as long as you have the galleons to pay for them.

The Apothecary along Diagon Alley is where you shop for the additional ingredients you need to mix potions. You can return here anytime by clicking the Diagon Alley icon within the gateway and then clicking the door to this shop.

As you'll discover, the Apothecary contains three shelves worth of ingredients. Each is displayed separately. You can view the different shelves within the shop by clicking the 1, 2, 3, or Next or Previous options near the bottom center of the screen.

Wizarding Tip

While visiting the Apothecary, when you click the name of an ingredient a pop-up window shows a description of the item, how many of the items you currently own, and its price. You also see a blue Buy button you can click to purchase more of that item.

Don't waste galleons purchasing ingredients you don't need or that you already own plenty of. You can always come back later to the Apothecary and purchase the additional ingredients you need, when you need them.

As you continue on within your Pottermore adventure, you find and are able to collect additional ingredients along the way, without having to purchase them.

REPLENISH YOUR INGREDIENTS WITHOUT HAVING TO BUY THEM

During your Pottermore adventure, when you find and collect a potion ingredient it is added to your trunk. However, when you use it up by brewing a potion, you need to replace that ingredient.

Instead of purchasing the ingredient from the Apothecary (and using up galleons), you can return to the exact book, chapter, and scene within your Pottermore adventure where you first found the ingredient and re-collect it, for free, an unlimited number of times. (You need to return to the location within Pottermore each time you use up that ingredient. You cannot stock up during a single return visit to a location.)

POTION BREWING FOR FUN AND TO EARN HOUSE POINTS

In addition to the potions you're required to brew as part of your main Pottermore adventure, after you unlock the Potions area you can click the Potions icon within the gateway at anytime and then brew potions to earn house points.

Before you can start brewing a potion, however, you must collect or purchase all the necessary ingredients. The potion book you're using, such as *Magical Drafts and Potions*, provides a list of exactly what you need for each potion.

Wizarding Tip

Brewing potions successfully requires several important steps. First, you need to collect or purchase all the necessary ingredients. Then, you need to follow the step-by-step directions within the potion book exactly as you mix together the right amount of each ingredient.

Next, it's necessary to brew the potion within a cauldron at just the right temperature and for the ideal amount of time. You also need to use your wand when instructed to add the perfect touch of magic.

By the way, it's also necessary to race against the clock (well, actually, it's a sand-filled hourglass) to complete each potion within a specific time limit; otherwise, it fails.

Achieving success requires practice, forces you to work at a steady pace and utilize perfect timing, and tests your ability to read and follow directions.

When you click the Potions icon within the gateway, the Potions page appears. Near the top center of this page, just under the Potions heading, are four options: Potion Book, Brewed, Cauldrons, and Ingredients.

- Click the Potion Book option to view a list of potions you're currently able to brew, based on how far along within your Pottermore adventure you've progressed.

- Click the Brewed option to see a list of potions you've successfully brewed already.

- Click the Cauldrons option to see a list of the cauldrons you own, and then choose which one you want to use for a specific potion. When you are viewing your cauldrons, each has a Use This Cauldron button below it. Click this button to select it. You also have the option to send a cauldron as a gift to someone else by clicking the Send as Gift button.

- Click the Ingredients option to view a complete list of ingredients you currently have at your disposal. This includes ingredients you've already purchased, ingredients you've found and collected during your Pottermore adventure, and ingredients that other people have sent you as a gift.

The Potions page within Pottermore is where you initially prepare to brew potions and gather the ingredients and equipment that you need.

Wizarding Tip

You can send any ingredient in your possession as a gift to someone else. However, do not give away rare ingredients that you can only find and collect during your adventure and not purchase within the Apothecary; otherwise, you might wind up being unable to complete an important potion later without having to retrace your steps and return to specific scenes.

Wizarding Tip

To stock up on new ingredients or replenish your supply, from the Potions page click the Buy Ingredients from Diagon Alley button (on the right side of the page) to visit the Apothecary along Diagon Alley.

You can also click the Diagon Alley icon within the gateway to return to this location, and then click once again on the Potions icon to return to the Potions page.

When you use an ingredient for a potion, it is removed from your trunk and must be replaced if you need more of that ingredient later.

PREPARE TO BREW A POTION

When you're ready to begin brewing portions (and earn house points for doing this successfully), click the Potions icon within the gateway to access the Potions page.

On the Potions page, click the Potion Book option. This provides a detailed listing of the potions you're currently able to brew and ingredients list for each potion.

As you're looking at the ingredients list, under the Key Ingredients heading, each ingredient is listed separately. If you see a check mark to the left of the listing, you already have the required ingredient (and the right amount of it). However, if you see a Buy button to the left of the listing, you need to purchase that ingredient before you can brew the potion.

So, if you see all check marks next to the list of required ingredients, you're ready to brew the potion. A Brew This Potion button appears to the left of the ingredients list.

As you can see, the Antidote to Common Poisons and Cure for Boils are both ready to be brewed; all the ingredients have been collected. The Brew This Potion button is displayed for both of these potions. However, the ingredients needed for the potions listed to the right have not all been acquired, so none of those potions can currently be brewed.

Wizarding Tip

You earn house points for each potion you successfully brew, but you lose house points each time you fail at brewing a potion. Seriously consider practicing the Cure for Boils potion before trying any others.

This is a practice potion that you can try as often as you want with no negative consequences if you fail.

To try brewing the Cure for Boils, click the Practice Brewing Cure for Boils button on the Potions page, after you click the Potion Book option. The necessary ingredients for this potion are provided.

From the Potions page, click the Potion Book option, and then choose which potion you want to try brewing. You can select the Cure for Boils anytime, or you can choose any other potion that has a Brew This Potion button associated with it.

GET STARTED BREWING A POTION

When you click the Practice Brewing Cure for Boils button, or the Brew This Potion button associated with any other potion, the Brew a Potion page appears. The first thing you see is the recipe for that potion and the brewing instructions from the appropriate page within your potion book.

Magical Warning

After you begin brewing a potion, you have only a limited amount of time to complete it successfully. You notice an hourglass on the left side of the Brew a Potion screen. When the sand in the hourglass all reaches the bottom, you have run out of time. If the potion isn't completed, it fails.

Wizarding Tip

To save valuable time, either memorize the list of steps required to brew the potion or write them down, in order, on a separate sheet of paper. Otherwise, you waste valuable time having to click the Potions book repeatedly to review the brewing directions.

Another option is to open a separate browser window, sign in to Pottermore twice (once using each browser window), and then leave the potion book displayed in one window while you brew the potion in the other browser window. This allows you to refer back to the potion book while you're brewing the potion, without wasting time.

Open two separate browser windows to display the potion book (right) and be able to brew a potion at the same time (left).

To successfully brew a portion, it is absolutely essential that you follow the steps outlined within the potion book in order and perform each step accurately. During the potion-brewing process, you stand in front of a table. On the table is everything you need to successful brew the potion. You have several tools at your disposal, including the following:

- **Cauldron**: This is the large pot in which you mix and brew your ingredients.

- **Cauldron spoon**: Placed within the cauldron is a large spoon that you use to stir your potion, as directed. Click the spoon's handle and drag it around to stir your potion.

- **Heat source**: Your cauldron is already positioned on top of a hot plate used to heat up and brew your potion. However, you need to turn on and off the heat and adjust the temperature as you're instructed to. To do this, click the orange or red buttons to turn on the heat and use the blue button to turn off the heat.

Wizarding Tip

Most potions require a certain amount of heat for a specific about of time. A meter helps you determine the correct temperature you need to maintain.

Use the orange (middle) heat control button to turn on and maintain a low flame. Click the red (right) button to turn on and maintain a high flame. Use the blue button to turn off the flame and allow the contents within the cauldron to cool down.

It's often necessary to turn on and off the heat controls or change the temperature (by switching between low and high heat) multiple times while brewing a single potion. Use the meter that appears to help you gauge and maintain the proper temperature for the correct amount of time.

Wizarding Tip

You can leave the heat turned on at the correct temperature for up to twice the amount of time that's instructed before the cauldron overheats. However, leaving a potion cooking for too long wastes valuable time. As soon as the timer shows you've reached the perfect cooking time, turn off the heat and move on to the next step.

When you achieve the right temperature, a timer appears so you can determine how long to keep that temperature steady before turning off the heat. For example, the recipe says, "Heat the mixture to 250 for 10 seconds."

Magical Warning

If you give your potion too much heat or leave the fire on for too long, you could melt your cauldron and then need to replace it by purchasing another one. When this happens, the potion you were attempting to brew fails.

- **Ingredients**: All the necessary ingredients for each potion are laid out for you on the right side of the table, in front of the potion book. Use your mouse to pick up and move each ingredient, one at a time, between the right side of the table, the mortar and pestle, and the cauldron. When moving items to the mortar and pestle, don't accidentally hit the cauldron. You need to move the ingredients up and over the cauldron to place them into the mortar and pestle.

- **Magic wand**: Although it might be hidden behind some of the ingredients on the table, you can always find the magic wand on the right side of the table, behind the ingredients, but in front of the potion book. You need it to complete every potion, so be ready to grab it at the right time and give it a wave.

- **Mortar and pestle**: These tools are used to crush up ingredients and turn them into powder before adding them to the cauldron. If the directions call for it, place the necessary ingredients into the mortar (which is the stone bowl to the left of the cauldron), and then use your mouse to control the pestle and crush the ingredients.

For example, in the directions for the Cure for Boils, Step 1 involves adding six snake fangs into the mortar. You're then instructed to crush them into powder. To do this, grab one snake fang at a time from the right side of the table and place it into the mortar.

Each time the ingredient lands in the mortar, a small number appears to the left of the mortar. After you move all six snake fangs into the mortar, click the pestle repeatedly until the meter turns from red to green. When the meter turns green, the task is complete, and you're ready to move the ingredient into the cauldron, as instructed.

After the required ingredient is placed into the mortar, use the mouse to control the pestle and smash up the ingredient into powder. The meter starts off red (shown here), but it turns green when the process is done.

- **Potion book**: As you're brewing a potion, the potion book you're working from is always available from the right side of the table (if you don't have a second browser window open to the potion book). Click it to reread the directions for a potion. Keep in mind that the hourglass does not stop when you do this, so referring back to the potion book repeatedly wastes valuable time!

Wizarding Tip

Each time you successfully complete a step as you're brewing a potion, if you refer back to the potion book that step is crossed off. This is a good way to see whether you've completed a specific task correctly. However, don't get into the habit of constantly checking the potion book or you waste too much time and aren't able to complete the desired potion.

- **Hourglass**: On the shelf behind the table (to the left), you see the sand-filled hourglass. As soon as you begin mixing the potion, the timer starts. When the sand in the hourglass runs out, you're out of time and the potion fails. A circular timer appears and counts down the last 10 seconds you have before the sand runs out.

Wizarding Tip

As you're placing ingredients on the right side of the table into the mortar or the cauldron, sometimes you're able to grab several of the same items at once. Keep an eye on the Number icon when you place something into the mortar or cauldron to determine how many of that particular item you're transferring. For example, a recipe might call for 10 drops of an ingredient, but each time you place that item into the cauldron or mortar it might count as 2 drops. So, you only have to move ingredients 5 times, not 10. Each ingredient, however, is handled and measured differently.

Some potions take only a few minutes to complete from start to finish. Others, however, require that you leave them simmering over the fire for an hour or longer. If this is the case, you can exit out of the Potions area of Pottermore, or leave the website altogether, and then return at the appropriate time to finish up the potion. There's no need to sit there and watch it brew for extended periods, unless the recipe for the potion tells you otherwise.

While a potion is actually brewing, you see a Brewing option appear within the page of the Potions book. Click this to view a timer. Click the Next button to return to the potions table when something requires your attention.

THE NUMBER OF HOUSE POINTS YOU EARN DEPENDS ON THE POTION YOU BREW

After you begin brewing potions, you discover that some are much easier to complete successfully than others. However, you're rewarded more handsomely with house points for successfully brewing the more difficult potions.

A Message from Your Owl

The most house points you can lose as a result of failing to brew a potion is five. However, this maximum deduction is taken only if you manage to melt or blow up your cauldron. Otherwise, you are penalized a fewer number of points if the potion fails for another reason.

Brewing potions is a great way to practice becoming a better witch or wizard, plus you're able to earn valuable house points for your house. Who knows, maybe we'll see your Pottermore username displayed on your house's leaderboard sometime soon.

VI

MAKING FRIENDS WITH FELLOW WITCHES AND WIZARDS IN POTTERMORE

After the Sorting Hat places you within Gryffindor, Ravenclaw, Hufflepuff, or Slytherin, you become part of that house, and one of your goals is to earn as many house points as you can for your house. During your visits to Pottermore, however, you can also keep tabs on the progress of your housemates and your other online friends within Pottermore.

After you've added someone as your friend within Pottermore, you can exchange gifts or challenge others to a Wizard's Duel.

INVITE PEOPLE TO BE YOUR ONLINE FRIENDS

Inviting people to be your online friend is easy. From the gateway along the top of the screen, click the Friends icon. The first time you do this, you see this message: You don't have any friends on Pottermore yet. If you know someone, why not add that person as a friend?

Within the empty field just below this message, enter someone else's Pottermore username, and then click the Add Friends button.

Magical Warning

The only way to make contact with other people within Pottermore is by using their username, not their muggle name. It's important that you never reveal your real name to the people you interact with online as you post public comments. When you post a comment, everyone on Pottermore can read it.

As soon as you enter someone's username, the Pottermore website locates that person and displays his username, animal avatar (pet), his house, when he joined Pottermore, how many house points he's earned, and what country he's from. If a green dot appears near the icon for his animal avatar, this indicates the person is currently online (and potentially available for a Wizard's Duel). Click the Add as a Friend button to confirm that you want to add this person as your friend.

Add as a Friend button

If you enter a valid username for someone, a Friend Found message appears. Click the Add as a Friend button below the person's username.

A Friend Request is then sent to the other person. When the other person approves your request, you and he then become online friends. After you've added at least one friend, a listing of your friends shows whenever you click the Friends icon.

ACCEPT INCOMING FRIEND REQUESTS

When you look up at the gateway and notice that a Number icon has appeared to the right of the Messenger Owl perched on the Spells icon, this means you have new notifications. (The number indicates how many notifications you have waiting.)

Click the owl to see your Notifications. If a Your Friend Requests message appears under the Friends heading, either click the Go to Friend button on the Notifications screen or click the Friends icon within the gateway to accept your new friend requests.

After clicking the Messenger Owl, you're notified when you have new friend requests.

As you're looking at your list of new friend requests, for each request you have the option of clicking the green Accept button to accept the friend request or clicking the red Ignore button to ignore the request.

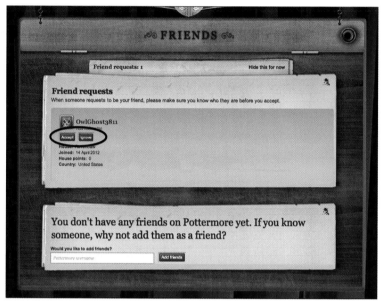

If you click the Accept button for a friend request, that person immediately becomes your online friend and appears on your Friends list.

HOW TO INTERACT WITH YOUR POTTERMORE FRIENDS

While looking at your Friends list, you see three buttons under each person's username: Challenge, Send Gift, and Remove Friend. If you want to challenge that person to a Wizard's Duel, click the Challenge button.

A Message from Your Owl

As you're viewing your Friends list after clicking the Friends icon, just under each friend's username is an option to Add Nickname. If you click this option, you're given the chance to type in your own nickname for that person. Here, you can enter their real-life name, if you know it. Doing this helps you keep track of the identities of your real-life friends within Pottermore.

The friends listed on your Friends list display in alphabetic order based on their Pottermore username. However, if you manually enter a nickname for each friend, you can then click the View By option near the top-right corner of the Friends screen and select Nickname. By doing this, your Friends list is re-sorted and displayed alphabetically based on the nicknames you've created for each of your friends.

Wizarding Tip

If you become friends with a lot of people on Pottermore, your list of friends will get long. To quickly move around this list, click the letter tabs along the right side of the Friends list. If you click the letter *O*, for example, and your friends are being sorted by their username, all your friends whose usernames begin with the letter *O* are displayed.

To access your Friends list at anytime, click the Friends icon within the gateway. You can also access your profile page and then scroll down to the center of it where you see the Friends heading. Click the View and Manage button. Or when you receive a new friend request, click the Messenger Owl, and then click the Go to Friends button.

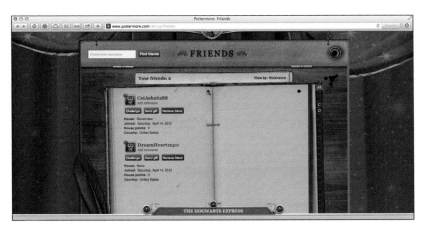

When looking at your Friends list, you can challenge someone to a Wizard's Duel, send a gift, or remove someone as a friend.

Wizarding Tip

See Section IV, "Wizard's Duels: Enhance Your Spell-Casting Skills," to discover strategies for becoming an expert when it comes to casting spells and winning duels. Remember, for every duel you win, you earn house points.

Although you cannot send private emails or instant messages to other Pottermore users, you can post public comments that your friends are able to read. A comment can include your thoughts, ideas, or boasts about your achievements.

A Message from Your Owl

Be sure to see Section VII, "Your Adventure Continues," for more information about posting comments on Pottermore.

HOW TO FIND NEW POTTERMORE FRIENDS

One way to find new friends is to read the chapter summary screen each time you complete a chapter. From these screens, you have the Add a Comment option. When you post a comment, everyone else is able to read it. It's also possible to read comments posted by other people.

A Message from Your Owl

You can post a comment from numerous other screens within Pottermore and read other persons' comments. For example, you can scroll down toward the bottom of the Great Hall, the Common Room, or any description for a character, place, book or creature, and post or read comments on these pages as well. The person's username who posted each comment is always shown.

As you're reading other peoples' comments, their Pottermore username is highlighted in yellow. Click a username to view her profile page. Then, near the top center of her profile page, her username, online status, how long she's been a Pottermore member, and her country are shown. Just below this information is an Add as a Friend button.

Wizarding Tip

Anytime you see someone's username displayed anywhere within Pottermore, you can also hover your mouse over it to display a small pop-up information box. This box includes that person's username, online status, avatar animal, house, when she joined Pottermore, how many house points she's earned, and what country she's from. An Add as a Friend button is also shown.

Click the Add as a Friend button that appears on someone's profile page to send him a friend request, even if you don't know that person in real life. You can become friends with other people from your house or with people from other houses. When it comes to participating in Wizard's Duels, you want to challenge people from other houses; otherwise, it's just considered practice.

Wizarding Tip

Whenever you visit the Common Room, on the right side of the screen is a leader board that displays the Pottermore users who have earned the most house points for your house. Click a username to view another person's profile page, and then click the Add as a Friend button to send that person a friend request.

When you visit the Great Hall by clicking the Great Hall icon within the gateway, you see leader boards for each house that displays the Pottermore users who have earned the most house points for their house. Click any of the usernames you see displayed to view their profile page, and then click the Add as a Friend button to send a friend request.

One reason why you might want to become online friends with those who have earned their way onto a Pottermore leader board is so that you can challenge them to Wizard's Duels and enhance your skills as a witch or wizard.

SENDING AND RECEIVING GIFTS

One thing you can do while viewing your Friends list is to send other people gifts. To do this, click the Send Gift button under someone's username. When you click the Send Gift button, a Send a Gift to a Friend pop-up window appears.

The name of the person you've selected to send the gift also shows within the pop-up window. From the pull-down menu, select what type of gift you want to send. Your have these gift options:

- Objects
- Chocolate frog cards
- Books
- Potion ingredients
- Cauldrons

After you choose a gift category, a list of related items that are currently stored in your trunk (that you've collected or purchased) display. Click what you want to send, and then click Send Gift.

You can also send a gift directly from your trunk. To do this, click the Trunk icon within the gateway. As you view the contents of your trunk, items that you can send as a gift have a Send as Gift button below them. Click this button to send the item. When you do this, a pop-up window shows the gift you've selected. From the Choose a Friend pull-down menu, select which friend you want to send the gift to, and then click Send Gift.

A Message from Your Owl

When you send gifts, recipients receive a notification from the Messenger Owl on their screen. What you sent as a gift is automatically removed from your trunk and placed into their trunk.

Likewise, if someone sends you a gift, you receive a notification from the Messenger Owl, and the gift that was sent appears within your trunk automatically. You can then access that gift by clicking the Trunk icon within the gateway.

Magical Warning

Don't give away objects, chocolate frog cards, books, potion ingredients, or cauldrons that you might need for you own adventure or to brew your own potions, unless you have duplicates or the ability to purchase replacements from Diagon Alley.

Because you might need some items you find during your adventure within Book 1 as you progress through later parts of Pottermore, it's a good strategy to give away only those items you can easily replace with a trip back to Diagon Alley, such as potion ingredients, as long as you have enough galleons.

SHOW OTHERS WHAT YOU LIKE ABOUT POTTERMORE

Displayed on the chapter introduction and chapter summary screens (as well as within descriptions for everything under the Read About section and on all the items you find during your adventure), you see a Like button with a thumbs-up icon displayed along with it.

Click the Add to Favorites button or the Like option when you discover something interesting in Pottermore.

Click the Like option to add whatever you're viewing to the list of things you especially like about Pottermore. You can also view how many other people also like the same thing as you.

In addition to using the Like option, it's easy to create and maintain your own detailed list of your favorite things about Pottermore. To do this, click the Add to Favorites button whenever you encounter something you really like. When you do this, that character, creature, place, object, potion, spell, or chapter (location) is added to your Favorites list.

Wizarding Tip

Click the Favorites icon within the gateway to view your Favorites list, which is sorted by category. Click a category tab to view what you've added as a favorite within that category.

When someone views your profile page, they can see the things that you have selected as your favorites under the Favorites heading. Likewise, when you look at other people's profile pages, you can see what they have selected as their favorite elements of Pottermore as well.

Keep in mind that you can send gifts, challenge friends to a Wizard's Duel, post comments, or "like" various aspects of Pottermore at anytime during your adventure. You can also click any of the unlocked gateway icons to transport yourself to places like Diagon Alley, Gringotts, the Great Hall, or the Common Room.

VII

YOUR ADVENTURE CONTINUES

If you've completed Book 1, *Harry Potter and the Sorcerer's Stone*, within Pottermore, you should be feeling really good about yourself right now. You rock! However, your adventure is only just beginning.

Throughout your journey through Pottermore, you're encouraged to post public comments that contain your ideas, suggestions, details about your accomplishments, or friendly taunts targeted to members of other houses. You're also welcome to upload your original Harry Potter-themed drawings and artwork to share them with other fans.

HOW TO POST COMMENTS ON POTTERMORE

Every time you complete a chapter within Pottermore and view its chapter summary page, you have the opportunity to add a comment. To do this, simply type your comment into the Comment field and click the Submit button. Within a short time, your comment is published on the page you posted it on.

Share your excitement about finishing a chapter within Pottermore or about something interesting you've discovered by posting a comment.

Also, feel free to enjoy reading comments from other people; you can find these displayed below the Comments heading. Click the House option to view comments written exclusively by your housemates, or click the Everyone option to view the comments posted on that page from witches and wizards from all the houses and from all over the world.

Wizarding Tip

You can also post comments at the bottom of The Great Hall page, on your house's Common Room page, or at the bottom of any page related to a character, place, book, object, or creature that you can read more about.

WHAT TO WRITE IN YOUR COMMENTS

You can write just about anything in your comments as long as it relates to Pottermore, Harry Potter, and is polite. Topics you can post comments about include the following:

- What you think about the chapter or scene in Pottermore that you just completed.
- Your accomplishments during your adventure.
- Your favorite Harry Potter characters or creatures.
- You can invite people to add you as a friend, so you can challenge them to Wizard's Duels.
- Ideas you have for improving Pottermore.
- Share strategies or tips that you've discovered.
- Friendly taunts to members of other houses about who can earn the most house points.
- Thoughts you have about the original content that J.K. Rowling included within Pottermore.

EVERY COMMENT AUTOMATICALLY INCLUDES CERTAIN INFORMATION

Whether you're posting a new comment or reading other people's comments, you can see the commenter's animal avatar, Pottermore username, and actual comment. To view details about a commenter, hover the mouse over her username when reading a comment.

If you look below each comment, you can see when it was posted; below that, there's a Like button, which you can click if you like what a particular person has to say.

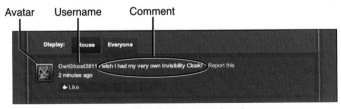

This is what a typical comment looks like after it's posted on Pottermore.

WHAT NOT TO INCLUDE IN YOUR COMMENTS

You should not post comments about some things. For example, never include your real name, email address, details about where you live, your phone number, your friends' muggle names, or any personal information about yourself. Also, being mean, rude, or writing anything that's inappropriate or offensive, or not related to Harry Potter or Pottermore isn't tolerated.

A Message from Your Owl

A Report This option appears to the right of every comment. Click this option only if someone posts a comment that's offensive, mean, inappropriate, or if it has nothing whatsoever to do with Pottermore or Harry Potter.

Keep in mind that all the comment pages within Pottermore are moderated. This means that the Pottermore Moderation Team first reads and approves each comment before it gets posted online. This process usually takes just a few minutes, but it's done for everyone's privacy and protection.

Remember, when posting comments, only Pottermore usernames are used; never include your muggle name.

SHARE YOUR ORIGINAL DRAWINGS AND ARTWORK

Everyone is welcome and encouraged to create a drawing or piece of original artwork, scan it into their computer, and then upload it to Pottermore, where it is published in an online gallery for fans from all over the world to see.

A Message from Your Owl

After uploading an original piece of artwork to Pottermore, it must be approved by the Pottermore Moderation Team before it gets published online. This process usually takes just a few minutes, but it could take up to several hours. So, be patient.

The artwork you upload to Pottermore can be a drawing, painting, or other scanned piece of original art that you create. It can be in black and white or full color, but it must somehow relate to Harry Potter or Pottermore, and it cannot be a digital photo or scanned photograph. If the Pottermore Moderation Team finds the content of your artwork inappropriate or offensive, it is not published online.

You can upload your artwork to Pottermore anytime you see an Add a Drawing button. These are typically located on the description pages for characters, places, objects, books, spells, and creatures.

Wizarding Tip

On the pages of Pottermore that include art galleries, scroll down toward the bottom of the page, below the Comments area, to view the artwork that other people have posted. You see a Drawings and Pictures heading with a few recently uploaded drawings displayed.

Click the See More option to view more artwork, or click the Add a Drawing button near the bottom of the page to upload your own artwork.

HOW TO UPLOAD ARTWORK TO POTTERMORE

The first step is to grab some pencils, pens, markers, paint, and some paper (or any other art supplies you need) and to create an original piece of artwork, such as a drawing or painting that has something to do with Harry Potter or Pottermore. You can also create original art from scratch using a painting or drawing program on your computer or tablet.

Next, use your computer's scanner to scan your artwork and create a digital file from it. You might need help from your parents for this step.

Wizarding Tip

When converting your artwork into a digital file, the file size must be less than 5MB, and it needs to be saved in the PNG, GIF, or JPG (JPEG) file format. The software you use with your computer's scanner offers the necessary options to create a compatible file.

After you save the artwork file in a compatible digital format (PNG, GIF, or JPG) on your computer (or on a storage device connected to your computer, such as an external hard drive or USB flash drive), return to Pottermore and decide where you want to publish your artwork. Each Pottermore description page for a character, place, object, book, spell, or creature, for example, has its own art gallery near the bottom of the page.

As you're working your way through your Pottermore adventure, within any scene, click any of the options listed below the Read About sign on the left side of the screen.

You can upload your own artwork to any description page for a character, place, object, book, spell, or creature, for example, that you can access from under the Read About sign on the left side of the screen during your adventure.

Scroll down on the description page for what you clicked. Located below the Comments section on the page, you see the Drawings and Pictures section. Click the Add a Drawing button.

You then see this message: Select a drawing to upload—no photos, just your own artwork please! Click the Browse button to locate your artwork file on your computer (or on an external storage drive or device connected to your computer), and then click the Upload button.

After clicking an Add a Drawing button, this is what you see. Click Browse to choose a file from your computer, and then click the Upload button.

The upload process takes up to several minutes. Then, allow a little while for the Pottermore Moderation Team to look at and approve your artwork. After that, it's published on the Pottermore page you uploaded it to.

If you have trouble deciding what type of artwork to create, consider drawing a picture of your favorite Harry Potter character or creature, or re-create a scene from the Harry Potter books or from Pottermore. Use your imagination!

PREPARE YOURSELF FOR BOOK 2, *HARRY POTTER AND THE CHAMBER OF SECRETS*

Book 2, *Harry Potter and the Chamber of Secrets*, has recently been unlocked within Pottermore and is full of new places to explore, adventures to experience, items to find, and mysteries to unravel. This adventure kicks off in Chapter 1, "The Worst Birthday." This first chapter contains two scenes.

This is what you see at the start of Book 2, Scene 1, "The Magic Word." Zoom in once to step inside the Dursley's house on Privet Drive. Some things look familiar, but on Harry's "bedroom" door below the stairs, you discover a lock.

In the months and years to come, Pottermore will continue to unlock new areas that correspond to each of the incredible books in the Harry Potter series.

After you make your way through Book 1 and Book 2, or at anytime during your adventure, you can revisit areas within Pottermore that you've already completed, and then read or reread the exclusive content written by J.K. Rowling. Plus, you can post your own comments, "like" specific things, or add things to your Favorites list.

Of course, you can also return to Pottermore as often as you want to help your house earn additional house points by participating in Wizard's Duels or by brewing potions.

A Message from Your Owl

To stay up to date on the latest developments related to Pottermore, be sure to read the *Pottermore Insider*. Visit http://insider.pottermore.com or click the *Pottermore Insider* link at the bottom of every Pottermore page.

You can also follow Pottermore on Twitter (@pottermore).

Index

C

X-Z

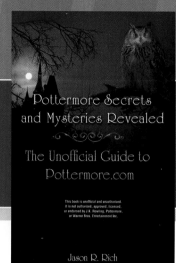

Pottermore Secrets and Mysteries Revealed

The Unofficial Guide to Pottermore.com

This book is unofficial and unauthorized. It is not authorized, approved, licensed, or endorsed by J.K. Rowling, Pottermore, or Warner Bros. Entertainment Inc.

Jason R. Rich

Safari
Books Online

FREE
Online Edition

Your purchase of *Pottermore Secrets and Mysteries Revealed* includes access to a free online edition for 45 days through the **Safari Books Online** subscription service. Nearly every Que book is available online through **Safari Books Online**, along with thousands of books and videos from publishers such as Addison-Wesley Professional, Cisco Press, Exam Cram, IBM Press, O'Reilly Media, Prentice Hall, Sams, and VMware Press.

Safari Books Online is a digital library providing searchable, on-demand access to thousands of technology, digital media, and professional development books and videos from leading publishers. With one monthly or yearly subscription price, you get unlimited access to learning tools and information on topics including mobile app and software development, tips and tricks on using your favorite gadgets, networking, project management, graphic design, and much more.

Activate your FREE Online Edition at
informit.com/safarifree

STEP 1:   Enter the coupon code: XODBYYG.

STEP 2:   New Safari users, complete the brief registration form. Safari subscribers, just log in.

If you have difficulty registering on Safari or accessing the online edition, please e-mail customer-service@safaribooksonline.com